Reflections on
ASIA

Books by Dr Mahathir Mohamad

Collected Speeches

MAHATHIR MOHA

Reflections on
ASIA

Pelanduk
Publications
www.pelanduk.com

Published in 2002 by
Pelanduk Publications (M) Sdn. Bhd.
(Co. No: 113307-W)
12 Jalan SS13/3E, Subang Jaya Industrial Estate,
47500 Subang Jaya, Selangor Darul Ehsan,
Malaysia.

Jointly with Millennium Books (1221539-U)

Check out our website at *www.pelanduk.com*
e-mail: *mypp@tm.net.my*

Perpustakaan Negara Malaysia   Cataloguing-in-Publication Data

Mahathir bin Mohamad, Dato' Seri, 1925-
    Reflections on Asia / Dr Mahathir Mohamad.
    Includes Index
    ISBN 967-978-813-X
    1. Asia–Economic conditions. 2. Asia–Foreign relations.
    3. Asia–Politics and government. 4. Foreign exchange–Asia.
    5. Economic forecasting–Asia. 6. Foreign exchange future–Asia.
    I. Title.
    330.95

Printed in Malaysia

Dicetak oleh:
CETAKMURNI SDN BHD

CONTENTS

PREFACE

IT HAS BEEN two years since Malaysia introduced selective currency control. It was a challenge for me to make the decision. But I had no choice. Malaysia and its people must remain in control of our destiny. The West condemned us for implementing this control because it violates their sacred capitalist beliefs. However, after two years, it has been admitted that the control works and the Malaysian economy has revived more than we had expected. Now, even George Soros admits that we made the right decision.

Looking back, I must admit that the past two years have been the toughest years that I had to face as prime minister of Malaysia. Mainichi Newspapers of Japan asked me to write a monthly column during that time. As I was writing the column, I was also struggling to make the policy work. As I have mentioned before, we did not just introduce the selective currency control. Along with the control, we also did many other things, such as lowering interest rates so that businesses could survive, dealing with non-performing loans, refinancing banks, etc. We also held property sales campaigns to get rid of the large number of buildings left unsold by the economic recession. We promoted retail sales and the easy hire purchase of motor vehicles.

Everything seems to be pointed in the right direction now. But we have to make sure that the foundations are strong enough for the future generations. Malaysia has set a target to be a developed country by the year 2020. But at the same time, we would like to retain our values and customs and our way of life.

The world is dominated by Western values and practices. Take the media, for instance. In the Western media, freedom means the right not only to report on matters of interest but also to distort and lie in favour of Western hegemony. The Western media have abused the freedom they have been given. And they resent any criticism against these abuses. It is therefore difficult for a third world leader to be reported truthfully in the West.

I find the Japanese press more willing to give a fair account of Asian affairs. Of course, sometimes the Japanese press merely prints news from Western wire services. But at least they are able to see both sides of the picture.

Japan has been very helpful to Malaysia during the crisis. I believe Japan would do more but it is deliberately being prevented from doing so. I hope this book will help create better understanding of the relations between countries and people and that helping others to enrich themselves will help to enrich us in the end. Destroy others and we will destroy something of ourselves.

Dr Mahathir Mohamad
August 8, 2000

CHAPTER I

ASIA'S ROAD
TO RECOVERY

FOR SEVERAL hundred years, Asia was a continent without a future. There are many now who believe that we have seen the return of history; that Asia has once again become a continent with no future.

The sun has set. The dragons have been slain. The tigers have become extinct. We are all finished.

They could be right.

They will without doubt be proven right if we in Asia cannot now summon the enormous will and the profound creativity to reform, to rebuild to recover and to once again be fully re-vitalised.

If we fail to get all our people, all our corporations, organisations and institutions to respond adequately and heroically to the present crisis, we will go further downhill very, very fast. It will be the end of our hopes and aspirations, the end of East Asia's rush to keep our rendezvous with our rightful place in the family of nations.

But what is now to be done, if we are to keep our appointment with history?

There are today many experts and organisations dispensing

1

quick fixes, the economic equivalent of magic potions, that can quickly take us on the road to salvation.

Everyone knows about the tablets of stone descended from Mount Liberalism, the theology of the free market. We are told that everything will be fine so long as we liberalise, deregulate and open up.

Some are even more specific: all would be fine if we allow international capital complete freedom to do whatever it wishes, constrained only by the hand of magical market forces.

Some are even more tightly focused. With laser-like precision, they say that everything would be solved, a new tomorrow would dawn, if only we allowed foreign financiers to buy up our financial sector — especially our banks — so that we will have no banks or financial institutions of our own anymore.

I beg to differ from all these simplistic solutions. I believe that the road to our salvation does not lie with a simple theology. I believe we must be completely pragmatic, proceeding with a policy only if it yields the desired results. To me it does not matter if the cat is black or white. We must only make sure that it is wonderful at catching the rats.

What is required is not a single formula but a hundred different policies, approaches and actions.

There is not one single plan which will bring prosperity to all and every nation. In economics and national development, as in medicine, there is no one universal cure.

I believe that for policies and actions to work, they must fit the specific needs, the specific conditions, the specific circumstances.

Just as there was no single East Asian model for success before the Crash of '97, there is no single East Asian model for success post the Crash of '97. As in the past, while we can and must learn from each other's experiences, we will all have to devise our own individual winning formulas.

However, in order for these various formulas to do the

trick, I believe that they must have at least the following characteristics.

First, our massive recovery efforts must have a comprehensive perspective. We cannot afford to neglect political stability, social tranquillity and cohesion while focusing on economics. Unfortunately, there is now too much advice from economic and financial experts who do not seem to be aware that there is a world out there that goes beyond money and finance, who therefore do not even take the broader economic picture into their reckoning, still less the wider political and social ramifications.

If we neglect political stability, social tranquillity and cohesion, all our economic successes, all our developments may come to nothing as a result of political upheavals and social conflicts.

Second, assuming that we have a comprehensive perspective, we must ensure a clear and productive order of priorities. This is what strategic thinking is all about.

Clearly, doing everything humanly possible in order to ensure that imprudent foreign bankers are paid does not automatically seem to be a productive or sensible top-most priority when the payment is only possible by depriving people of jobs, withdrawing food subsidies and precipitating daily riots and street violence.

While foreign lenders must be paid at all cost, any attempt to help local banks or business will be regarded as a "bail out" and condemned for creating a most dangerous 'moral hazard' which would seriously damage the present and future health of our financial and economic systems. Why is helping a foreign bank not a "bail out" and will not cause a moral hazard is something that is difficult to understand? Are foreign banks run by saints who would be prudent even it being imprudent cost them nothing. Are they immune to moral haggard?

Third, there is obviously the imperative of focus, a tight focus. Resources will always be limited. We have therefore to concentrate them on achieving the most critical objectives. Although many things are very important, a few things, a surprisingly few strategic things in fact, are absolutely (for want of a better word) 'strategic'.

They are the keys that will unlock a hundred doors. We must all make sure that we concentrate our limited time and resources on finding and turning these few keys.

Fourth, there is a need for balance, especially between the demands of social development and welfare, political stability and cohesion and economic and financial objectives. There is also a need to balance especially between the short-term imperatives and the longer-term imperatives.

Fifth, I believe that we must not be blinkered. Nothing, no theory, no principle, no formula should be regarded so sacred that they cannot be critically examined, modified, changed or even discarded. We must be pragmatic. What counts is the result. We should not believe in proudly announcing that the operation is successful but the patient died.

Sixth, I believe that if we are to rapidly recover and restore a sustained and dynamic growth, fierce competitiveness and economic resilience, there is a need for a total national effort. The entire nation must be united. More, the entire nation must be fully mobilised, working as one organic whole, united behind a single purpose. This is where the societies of East Asia have a comparative advantage.

Many have argued that the Japanese people have not yet woken up to the fact that their economy is in a state of crisis, that a massive national effort will be needed if Japan is to once again be the dynamic powerhouse of East Asia.

This cannot be said for the Malaysian nation. Malaysians know we are in deep crisis. We know we have to reform, to rebuild, if we are to recover and once again be fully revitalised.

Since we went against economic orthodoxy and introduced selective currency controls on September 1, 1998, the Malaysian economy has retreated from the brink of utter disaster.

We have been able to reduce interest rates. So now our companies can start breathing again, and investing again. We have ensured liquidity, so that the engine of growth can now start purring again.

Since September 1 1998, the Kuala Lumpur Stock Exchange has been the number one performer in the world, more than doubling in price.

It is still too early to say that Malaysia is well on the road to recovery or that Asia will recover. But it is clear that most of us are on the mend.

I believe that almost all of us will find our way back to the road of dynamic growth — to resume our interrupted growth run.

CHAPTER 2

SMALL COUNTRIES
VS GIGANTIC POWER

THE INTERNATIONAL financial system was the main focus of the very successful Group of 15 Summit held in Montego Bay, Jamaica on February 10, 1999. The issue is a vital one as it has a great effect on developing countries.

It was the first time that such meetings have focused on the financial system and its prominence this time was because developing nations have real problems with it. Among the G-15 nations, Malaysia, Indonesia and Brazil have faced problems caused by currency traders and we know the consequences of having them attack our economies.

Many countries were eager to hear about how Malaysia handled the problem including currency controls and regulating the flow of short-term capital from other countries. Now, we appreciate better the kind of threat that can come with globalisation. We all agree that globalisation is something that has to happen. We cannot stop it. But on the other hand, it could be regulated in such a way that it will not harm national economies.

We need to have a dialogue with the North, or developed nations, in particular with the Group of 7, leading industrialised nations. We think that when the new international financial architecture is designed it should not be done only by the countries of G-7 or the Bretton Woods institutions such as the International Monetary Fund (IMF), the World Bank or Bank of International Settlement (BIS). Developing countries like Malaysia should have a say in changing the world financial system since we have faced the problems that it has caused. During the G-15 meeting, Venezuela was very keen to know about Malaysia's currency controls in detail. I explained how we prevented Malaysia's money from getting into the hands of the currency traders. The question was how do we pay for imports when we control the currency. In the case of Malaysia, I explained that we export more than we import. Therefore we earn sufficient foreign exchange to pay for our imports and even to pay our debts.

However, in the case of Latin American countries, the value of imports is much bigger than that of exports, so they must borrow money to pay for their imports. Because of this, when their currency is devalued they find themselves even more unable to pay. So it is quite difficult for them to emulate what Malaysia has done.

Brazil has taken a different course of action by accepting the IMF regime. Although we were attacked in the same way as Brazil has been, we have been able to resist the need to go to the IMF and we have regained control over our currency.

We in Malaysia have been discussing currency controls for quite a long time. Many of us were afraid that they would damage our economy. It was difficult to convince everybody that we need to have currency controls. Eventually everyone agreed that we have no other way out. Now we know that currency controls have been effective in stabilising our economy and getting it back onto the growth path.

Before attending the G-15 summit, I attended the World Economic Forum in Davos, Switzerland. I used to go there every year, but for the past 10 years other representatives from my country went there. These included Malaysia's former Deputy Prime Minister, Anwar Ibrahim, who was very popular as he always agreed with the Western views. Now that the Western countries are condemning us, I felt I should go to Davos to find out why. I wanted to have the opportunity to speak to them about our currency control. I found out that they did not know what kind of control we have imposed. Still many of the speakers in Davos were supportive of the idea of currency control. Their attitude has apparently changed. Many even expressed their objections to the IMF and the currency traders. The Canadian Prime Minister Jean Chretien spoke about "the young boys in red suspenders" trying to teach Governments how to run their countries. He obviously did not like to be told how to run his country by these youngsters who had never run Governments.

More people now support the Malaysian stand, so much so that a well-known Western magazine express the view that the rantings of Prime Minister Mahathir is now regarded as "conventional wisdom".

In a way, I am happy that many people in the West now understand our views on currency trading but we are still not getting anywhere regarding regulating currency trading. The United States, in particular, is still very much against any attempt to curb currency trading.

In Davos, I had the opportunity to meet senior editors of major Western newspapers and television networks. Some of them seem bent on making me out as anti-Jewish. Apparently mentioning that the currency traders are Jews and Europeans proves that I am anti-Jew. That Jewish firms such as Salomon Smith Barney and Goldman Sachs are advisers to the Malaysian Government is not regarded as disproving my being anti-Jew. There seem to be a desire to antagonise the Jews so that Malaysia will face difficulties in attracting investments or borrowing money.

In 1997 in Hong Kong at the World Bank-IMF meeting, I

blamed currency traders for the economic turmoil that we were suffering. Immediately, I was attacked for failure to understand the international financial market and the herd behaviour of the investors. Every time I criticised them, they pushed down the value of the Ringgit, almost as though to punish me. Some Malaysians also advised me not to talk against the currency traders because they can make things difficult for us.

Because of IMF pressure we had initially increased the rate of interest and squeezed credit for our businesses. The banks and the businesses were almost bankrupted. The Malaysian Government then decided to go against IMF's advice and impose currency control, reduce interest rates and increase liquidity. We were condemned by almost everyone. They said the economy would get worse or at best would only improve for a short while.

But today as we all know many experts have come round to the view that we are right on both counts. We did not disagree with the views of others simply for the sake of disagreeing. We may not be expert analysts and learned academics. But we have considerable experience in developing Malaysia, a multi-racial and potentially unstable country once dependent upon just two commodities, rubber and tin. We converted Malaysia into a middle-income country with 80 percent of its USD70 billion exports consisting of sophisticated electronic goods. Surely we must know something about running a country, developing it, and managing its finances. When we took a stand against currency trading and unrestricted short-term capital flows, we know what we are doing.

My deputy, Anwar Ibrahim, whom I had to remove recently was a populist. He likes to be praised especially by foreign VIPs. He is especially liked by his American counterparts because he always agrees with them. I am afraid I like to speak my mind and some of my views are not popular with foreigners. This is something that I cannot help.

In my student days, I was a rebel. I was not popular with my teachers. Even though I got good marks I did not get the right recommendations. I wanted to study law but I could not get a scholarship. When I was young we had to call all Europeans 'masters', in Malay 'Tuan'. We were always regarded as inferior to them. I always resented having to call other people master. I think in my own country I should be the master. We called them master out of politeness, but they assumed that when we called them master we thought of them as being our masters. Malaysia was not a full colony. We had our own governments, our own sultans (king). When the British came back after World War II, they wanted to make Malaysia a full colony. I organised protests against the proposed Malayan Union. I didn't want to be under other people's rule. I wanted to be independent. To be independent means not taking orders from others. If you are independent you must be free, to be able to say what you think.

Unfortunately, although the West advocates free speech, they don't like others to freely criticise them. It is also the same with globalisation and free flows across borders. While they insist on free flows of capital across borders they object to free flows of people, especially poor coloured people into their countries. Fairness and justice mean different things to them. I remember the case of a well-known golf course in California that was bought by the Japanese. The Americans sold it because they needed the money, but Japanese people could not become members of the golf club. For them it is fair, but if we do the same thing it is not fair.

The 21st century looks gloomy for the developing world. Unfortunately it is likely to be so unless the G-15 countries can influence the decisions of some countries of the north, such as those in Europe.

There is a deliberate attempt by the North to dominate the world economy. Oil companies, which were broken up into small companies, are now merging to become much bigger.

Automobile companies, too, are merging to become huge. All industries are becoming very, very big, because with their size they can dominate small industries like those in Malaysia. They attacked our stock market, causing the shares to go down, so that they can buy our companies cheap. In the end they will control our economy and our people. I am worried that we will lose our independence when that happens.

Politically, we may seem independent, but once we become economically dominated we will lose our political freedom as well. An example is the 'banana republics' of Central America. There, the economy is entirely dependent upon the revenue from bananas. The foreign owners of the banana plantations are able to influence the politics of these countries.

The only way we can prevent these things from happening is by working together. Japan should understand our problems. Japan is the world's second-biggest economy, so Japan should work together with us.

Before the recent meeting of G-7 finance ministers in Bonn, Germany, I wrote letters to all the leaders of G-7 countries, including U.S. President Bill Clinton. I asked that developing countries be consulted in the planning of a new world financial architecture. The G-15 nations should have a role in this process. As you know, the North has decided that only the G-7 and institutions like the IMF, the World Bank, BIS and others under their control will design the new architecture. We have no say. The solution is going to help them, not us. Japan, Germany, France, even Canada believe that some form of currency control is needed. However currency trading is done almost exclusively by U.S. firms. So until the United States agrees, there will be no new financial architecture.

I am also in favour of the idea drawn up by Japan to have an exchange rate band between the U.S. dollar and the yen or the euro. I flew to France on the way back from Jamaica, and met French President Jacques Chirac for two hours. He also agreed with this idea, he even went to the United States to push that idea. But, as you know, the resolution of that issue was vague. The Unites States says that everybody agrees not to regulate currency trading but others say that only the United States is against the idea. Currency trading benefits the U.S. So why should they regulate it?

In a bipolar world, capitalist countries had to be friendly or we would defect to the communist side. Now we cannot defect to the other side anymore. This will be so unless Japan and the EU countries decide to oppose the gigantic power of the United States. Japan can help if it disposes of the dollar bonds that it holds. Alternatively' Japan can make some money available to us.

CHAPTER 3

LIFE WAS
SCHOOL AND HOME

WHEN I went to university in Singapore, I was considered one of the luckiest students in Malaysia. At that time, very few people particularly indigenous people were able to go to university, and very few could get a scholarship, so I was fortunate to obtain one. Today there are thousands and thousands of scholarships available, both domestically and internationally. Students can study any subject as long as they have the capability to do so. The problem today is not the opportunity to study, but the desire of the person to get a better education or not. Sometimes a student gets a scholarship, but he doesn't study. They take the opportunity and scholarship for granted. They think that it is their right to go to university but not their responsibility to study. Some of them get involved in activities that distract them from concentrating on their studies. Some of them are more interested in politics. They believe that they know about how a country should be run. They spend a great deal of time demonstrating, or debating how the country should be governed. As a result, although they get the opportunity, they do not receive the amount of education that they should be getting.

I don't mind if students are interested in politics, but they shouldn't go to university just to become politically active. We spend public money to educate them. It's irresponsible to waste funds earmarked for education.

I was active in politics when I was in the university but that was when Malaysia was under foreign rule. I was struggling against colonial rule believing that independence would bring better educational opportunities. Now we are independent and should use our educational opportunities to gain good education. We spend 20 percent of the national budget for education, more than any other country. So for students there really is no reason to fight against the government. The expectations of my generation have been fulfilled. The status of the minister of education in our government is very high, because we think that education is the way to make our people upwardly mobile. If the country wants to progress, people must be educated. Some people believe that Japan places too much emphasis on education, creating a lot of tension. The family puts too much pressure on the child.

If, together with that you expose children to a way of life that is too free and lack decorum as in violent Western movies then they will follow such lifestyles as a way out of their stress. Of course, not everybody is like this, but there are those in every community whose ability to control themselves is minimal. Such people are easily influenced.

Families play a very important role in education. I attribute my own upbringing and education to my father, backed by my mother. Both were strong disciplinarians and keen on education. I liked to read when I was small. I was the class librarian when I was in Grade 4. Every weekend I bought magazines for the class. I would read all the stories in the magazines, maybe more than 30 stories over the weekend. There were magazines about Western films, adventure stories, detective stories, war stories from World War I. I wasn't an athlete, I didn't play games. I spent most of my time reading.

We had a big table in the living room in my house, where I, my brother and our cousins studied. When we heard my father coughed as he reached the gate on his way back from work, we would run to the table to study. Nowadays, children are not as easily influenced by their parents. They have their own ideas and watch television, so it is more difficult to be a parent than in my father's day. Then, we never went out of the house after coming back from school. We didn't go to friends' houses or to town. My father bought us a small bicycle, but we were not allowed to ride on the road. Life was school and home, and that was all. Although I was not as strict as my father, I did manage to influence my children sufficiently to study.

We are Muslim. There are many Islamic teachings that help us to have good character. To learn to respect parents and elders, to believe in God, not to do what is forbidden, this is the religious basis that will contribute to our children having better character. They all have to study the Koran.

Our culture doesn't tolerate open discussion about sex. So initially I wanted to avoid making the case of former Deputy Prime Minister Anwar Ibrahim public, if he were to resign quietly. However, for me it is more important that the person who may become the leader of this country has his character made known public. So the exposure is unavoidable, because he chose to fight. He wanted full publicity, for the trial to be conducted in English so that the foreign press could understand. It was his choice.

Modern Muslim children are exposed to the same thing as other children worldwide. In the Internet, for example, one can access pornography, so it is impossible to protect children from that. If we try to censor the internet, we are condemned by the whole world. The Internet is a sacred thing. So we must allow the children access to all kind of things including all kind of lies from irresponsible people. It is difficult for people to know what is true and not true.

Last year, the police arrested three people for spreading news via the Internet that there would be a riot in downtown Kuala Lumpur. In Malaysia we have different races. If you start playing with these differences, you can easily start fighting as witnessed in Bosnia, Kosovo and Northern Ireland. It is very dangerous. We would rather arrest such people than allow our country to become a killing field. Malays are Muslim, but Islam has lots of interpretations. Muslim politicians interpret Islam in order to justify what they are doing. This can be wrong. They want to do something that is not Islamic, but in order to gain people's acceptance, they say "This is Islamic". If this is said by religious leaders, people tend to believe it. In the 1400 year history of Islam, there have been many wrong interpretations of Islam. These wrong interpretations prevent Muslims from making progress and competing with other religious creeds. Islam gave strength to the Arabs when they first embraced it. So it is not the reason for Muslim backwardness.

Later on, Muslims became backward, because Islam was wrongly interpreted by people with objectives of their own. So what we try to do here is to go back to the real original interpretation of Islam, which was able to make the Arabs very progressive and established a very great civilisation.

Islamic teaching says that you may marry four wives. But that is not something you must do. Only in certain circumstances. When people go to war, men are killed and many women are widowed. Then there are more women than men. It is wrong for the women to be unmarried and have nobody to look after them. Before Islam, Arabs married many, many, many wives. If they had money they could marry 30. So when the Prophet Muhammad came, he told them that the number of permitted wives should actually be one, but allowed four. Islam says that you can have four wives if you can be just and fair to all, and that is impossible. This means that you can only marry one. I adhere to the teaching of Islam. My wife's father was head of the religious department in the State of Selangor. He made a ruling that to take a second or third wife, you must have the signature of the first wife. In that way less polygamy was practiced. He also backed the idea of women having careers in order to be independent. I had to wait several years for my wife to get her doctor's degree before marrying her.

To me, my family is very important. I like the office to be near my house, so that I can be close to my family. It takes me only five minutes to go home, so I always have lunch there. I believe in family values including extended family. Our children are grown up now and have separate homes, but we still get together quite often. Family gives a reason for living. I cannot imagine a person without a family. Family sort of anchors you to life. Otherwise you will be floating without any base.

My wife is a good partner and gives me full support. I talk with her about politics, but not much only something that is not official. In Malaysia, we always have plans and a target for the future. Vision 2020 is one example. This is a target to become a fully developed country. We have our own definition of being developed and it is not the same as Western definition. We want to have the same wealth, same technical capabilities, skills in management and administration as other developed countries. But, at the same time, we want to maintain our Asian value system and focus on good education. This helps us to have a common objective, to have faith in our ability.

We now have a Malaysian sailor who is attempting to sail around the globe by himself. People are thrilled with his adventure every day. They feel a sense of pride, which is good for the nation. However, we also have problems just like the developed countries. The word 'lepak' means young people who roam around aimlessly, doing nothing, just watching people passing by.

As we progress, this is bound to happen. The important thing is to keep our youth continuously excited and active. Moving goals is one way of doing this. If you achieve one goal, make another one. When you think there is nothing more to achieve you will die spiritually. It is necessary to be chasing after a target to be alive and excited.

When you have become rich, you lose interest and stop being grateful. All civilisation is like that. After you have reached the peak you will collapse. That was what happened to the Roman Empire. It is the same with the Muslim Empire. When they were motivated by religion, they wanted to acquire knowledge, study the works of the Greeks and Romans, translate them into Arabic. Europeans used to go to Muslim universities in Baghdad, Iraq, because they thought that they were the most advanced people. But the Muslims ceased to seek knowledge at that stage.

It is like the rich people who give all the hard work to the foreigners. If they do so, their muscles weaken. I worry that our people do not want to work. For example, some say that if Indonesians work in our plantations, we can pay less to them. But once you allow that to happen, eventually they will take over. We will be so dependent on them that we cannot do anything ourselves.

CHAPTER 4

LEADERS IN DEMOCRACY

FIRSTLY I would like to congratulate Mr. Shintaro Ishihara for his convincing win in the Tokyo gubernatorial election. Mr. Ishihara interviewed me and subsequently published a book entitled 'The Asia That Can Say No'; in which he expressed his views and mine separately in different chapters.

I admire Mr. Ishihara very much for his firmness and his outspokenness. I agree with a number of his views but not all. I find it difficult to appreciate his views on China for example.

His outspokenness and strong views differ very much from those of most Japanese leaders. The political system and practice in Japan probably prevent the emergence of strong leaders and this in turn affects Japan's credibility and leadership position in the world.

Prime Ministers in Japan do not hold their position for very long. Most serve only for two years. This short period prevents the Prime Ministers and their governments from being effective. In the past the civil servants really run the government.

It takes time for a Prime Minister or an executive President to even learn about his job. It takes much longer to formulate a policy, to implement it and to see it through. Consequently, little can be achieved if a leader is given only two years to be Prime Minister or President.

There is obviously a fear that if a leader holds the top position for too long he would become too powerful and would also become corrupt. This may be the general rule but it is not always true. Conscientious and patriotic leaders will not allow themselves to abuse their authority or to be corrupt.

The best way to judge a leader's integrity is through the results he achieves. Corrupt, power-crazy leaders almost invariably harm their countries. We need only to look at the record of dictators throughout history. Their countries may do well for a short while but invariably they go into regression. At best they remain static economically although the dictators may make a show of their success through various shows. Without exception the ordinary people would suffer.

We must avoid the possibility of a dictator emerging but our fear must not lead us into having ineffective leaders. The democratic system where leaders can be removed through the ballot box is sufficient guarantee that a popular leader can stay long enough to be effective, while one with a tendency to abuse power would be removed.

Unfortunately, even if a leader is effective and delivers on his promises, if he stays too long the other leaders are bound to get restless. These leaders will try to push aside the incumbent whether he is good or not.

A leader must accept that even if he has done well, he would still be pushed aside if he overstays his welcome. I fully subscribe to this view. However, a leader has a duty to ensure that his removal will not result in a totally unsuitable leader taking his place.

In Malaysia, we are at the moment having a problem because the designated successor who had been groomed to take over from the present Prime Minister was suddenly found to be totally unsuitable. He was found to have abused his authority in order to protect his personal interest. He had also committed other misdemeanours, which make him unsuitable to become the country's leader. He was therefore dismissed from the Government.

In Malaysia, as elsewhere, everyone is equal before the law. The fact that a leader is highly placed in the Government does not mean that the laws should not be applied to him. Accordingly, the former Deputy Prime Minister was charged and tried. Because of the interest shown in his case by locals as well as foreign people, the trial has set some kind of a record. It lasted more than 70 days. The defendant had a panel of nine lawyers to defend him. Members of the diplomatic corps, and the media, foreign and local were present in full force. The trial was conducted in English, as the defendant wanted the foreign media to follow the proceedings.

The verdict by the presiding judge is that the former Deputy Prime Minister is guilty of corruption on four charges. Each charge carries a sentence of six years; a total of 24 years. But the judge decided to make the sentences concurrent, thus reducing the sentence to six years. Normally in Malaysia this means serving only four years.

Immediately the Western media and Western governments condemned the verdict and the judiciary. Clearly had the verdict been in favour of the defendant, the judiciary would not be condemned.

The fact is that for many years now the Western media and some Western governments had been favouring Dato Seri Anwar and wants him to succeed the present Prime Minister quickly. When they find that the candidate cannot now become the Prime Minister, they are clearly furious. They did everything possible to disparage the present Malaysian Government and in particular the Prime Minister. They favoured Dato Seri Anwar with media support and cut out any good reports on the Malaysian Government and its supporters completely. Anwar's views were widely publicised, including his accusations that the present Government of which he was a member until recently, is corrupt and oppressive. The activities of his supporters including the riots staged by them were not only reported but also grossly exaggerated. The Western media and leaders of Western governments openly urged the people to riot and topple the Government by undemocratic means. Coming from the champions of democracy this is quite surprising.

Against these distortions of facts and adverse publicity, there is little the Malaysian Government or its supporters can do. It must be remembered that Malaysia is facing financial and economic turmoil due to the attacks by currency traders and stock market manipulators. These economic problems occupy much of the time and effort of the Malaysian Government leaders. The Government cannot attend to the misleading reports in the Western Press.

Worse still the foreign media and the Western governments use the economic problems of Malaysia to further undermine the support for the Government and to help Anwar's course. Everything is done to prevent Malaysia from achieving economic recovery so that the people would turn against the Government.

Fortunately, Malaysia has managed to recover economically. But the attack goes on and every effort is made to unseat the Malaysian Government. Their hope is to engineer the defeat of the National Front party in the coming general election.

Unless the Appeal Court overturns the verdict of the High Court, it looks like Anwar won't be able to contest in the next election. His wife, Wan Azizah has become his proxy and has been made the President of a new party set up by Anwar's followers. The hope is that if their party wins the election, Anwar might be released and pardoned. In which case he would be able to contest in a bye-election and become Prime Minister.

Malaysia is a developing country and has been independent only slightly over 40 years. A developing country cannot afford turbulent politics. It needs peace and stability for the Government to implement plans for economic development for the well being of the people.

Malaysia is a democratic country. Elections are held regularly since independence. The elections invariably results in a good number of seats being won by the opposition parties. In several instances, the opposition parties manage to defeat the governing party and set up governments in the states of the Federation. Kelantan, Terengganu, Sabah and Penang have had governments by parties other than the Barisan Nasional or National Front. In the case of Kelantan, the opposition party has won repeatedly and there is nothing the central Government can do to dislodge it.

Confrontation between the state government and the central Government as a result of political differences adversely affects the growth of the state. But if the people prefer a party that is against the central Government then they must be prepared for the consequences.

Despite the political differences and the confrontation between the political parties, the central Government has always been strong and has been able to ensure peace and stability in the country. But obviously Anwar does not like this. He believes that even if the majority prefers peace and stability he should disrupt it by resorting to violence, street demonstrations and a campaign of hate against the Prime Minister in particular and the Government in general. He has seen how such street demonstrations have been successful in overthrowing governments and leaders in other countries and he hopes the same thing will happen in Malaysia.

The majority of the Malaysians have so far not responded to this kind of tactic. Malaysians seem to prefer the democratic process and the will of the majority. Obviously the next election will show what this will is going to be like.

Malaysians generally like to have peace and stability. Weak governments and weak leaders cannot provide this. The quality of the leaders that they chose is important. Whether they can deliver on their promises is also very important.

Fortunately for Malaysia, in the 42 years of independence the people have been able to observe the performance of the different parties when they form governments. Of course some parties have never won enough seats to form governments because their extreme views are known and Malaysians reject extremism. Of the parties other than the National Front, which have set up governments in various states, none has been able to deliver on their promises. The states, which they govern, have not only failed to make progress but have actually retrogressed.

The only party that has contributed towards Malaysia's rapid progress and prosperity is the present ruling party, the Barisan Nasional which forms the central Government and the governments of majority of the component states of Malaysia. As the other parties have no track record to offer, they have resorted to a hate campaign against the leaders of the Government party, the National Front.

All kinds of lies are being spread about Government leaders. They are said to be corrupt, to have huge sums of money in foreign banks, and to have committed other kinds of misdemeanours.

Political leaders who resort to telling lies in order to win support may still win but their success will be a disaster for their country.

In a democracy, the people decide. But the people need to be informed and guided. The media play a big role but political leaders can and do shape the opinions of people. We would like to believe that the people would do what is right and what is good for them. But leaders can influence them to do wrong things and make wrong decisions. When leaders are bad and think only of their own ambitions, the people will decide wrongly.

Some people say the important thing is that the process is democratic. They forget that democracy was devised in order to ensure governments are good and responsible. In other words, democracy is meant to serve the people. But now it seems that the people must serve democracy at all cost. It is not that democracy is bad but politicians and political leaders have found ways of abusing democracy. More than ever people must learn to distinguish between good leaders and bad leaders.

CHAPTER 5

THE KILLING FIELDS

NATO'S ASSAULT on Yugoslavia cannot be avoided, if NATO wishes to maintain its claim that it will not tolerate human rights abuses. This is especially relevant in Europe, since the members of NATO have said that they do not recognise borders when it comes to human rights abuses. They claim a right to act even in other people's countries.

It is very clear that the Serbs are oppressing the ethnic Albanians in Kosovo. Otherwise, why would the Kosovars run away to Albania, to Macedonia, etc.

And the stories about people being killed, being massacred, the disappearance of more than 200,000 young men, all these things point to the kind of ethnic cleansing that the Serbs are well known for in Bosnia.

So, there is no doubt that Serbs were abusing human rights on a very grand scale. And anybody who speaks about human rights, and wants to uphold these rights must act and put a stop to such abuses.

NATO cannot just say that this is happening in an independent country when they have been acting against independent countries like Iran, Iraq, Libya, etc.

Here is a clear-cut case where they must act. Unfortunately they have taken a long time to act. Every hour, every day that they delay, more Kosovars were killed. For very many the decision to act came too late.

Despite the sophistication of their aerial attacks, there is no way they can defeat the Serbs without ground forces. The war in Vietnam proved this conclusively. The sooner they go in with ground forces the sooner will the Serbs be defeated.

As far as I am concerned, the action taken by NATO is right and the assault by NATO is necessary for there is no other way to stop Milosevic from murdering the Kosovars.

In Cambodia, because of the principle of non-interference two million people were killed. Only when the Vietnamese crossed the border into Cambodia to overthrow the Khmer Rouge regime was the killing stopped.

So, I would say that NATO's action is somewhat similar to the Vietnamese action in Cambodia where the Vietnamese acted and in the process stopped the massacre. However, the Vietnamese went in on the ground, and almost immediately the government was overthrown.

Fighting on the ground must result in loss of lives on both sides. The Vietnamese lost many lives and so must NATO if it is serious about defending human rights.

Unwillingness to commit ground troops must result in the Serbs getting away with oppression and ethnic cleansing once again. This will make nonsense of the claim that the Western liberal democrats will not allow abuses of human rights anywhere.

It is regrettable that the so-called pinpoint accuracy of NATO bombings can result in wrong targets being hit. This is happening too frequently and leads one to believe that the claim by Iraq that hospitals and milk factories were bombed could be right.

The explanation that the Chinese Embassy was hit because of wrong information is hard to believe. Surely the location of the Chinese Embassy must be known to about everyone who had been to Belgrade.

I can understand China's reaction after the bombing. Before the bombing, although they did not agree with it, they did not actively oppose it. However, now they have to actively oppose the bombing. It would be unnatural if they don't.

NATO must learn from its mistakes. When they make mistakes, they must be prepared to admit it. In Iraq, in Sudan, they hit the wrong targets. Big powers find it difficult to admit mistakes and apologise.

This is the problem. Powerful countries seem to think they can take the law into their own hands. They think they can ignore the views of other people.

The bombing of the Chinese Embassy is bound to affect the peace process. The Serbian government might feel encouraged that it now has support from China and Russia. So, the Serbs will not give in easily.

But difficult though it may be, there is no choice but to continue the attacks. The Serbs should not be allowed to indulge in ethnic cleansing with impunity. It is unthinkable that in this day and age people should kill innocent people and expel them from their country in pursuit of racial or national ambitions.

In Malaysia, we have a multiracial population and we do have racial problems. But we don't kill people and chase them out of the country as a way to solve our problems. Once of course, there was bad blood between the Malays and the Chinese and race riots did break out. But we resolved it through negotiations and accommodating each other. It takes time but it can be done. Today Malays and Chinese live side by side and work together. Every race in Malaysia is represented in the Government. For 30 years now there has been no ethnic confrontation or race riots.

The Serbs maintain that, historically, Kosovo belongs to them. If you go back into history, and try to claim the land that belonged to you in the past there would be endless wars. Everybody can claim everybody else's land. Malaysia could claim a lot of land that is now outside Malaysia but historically belonged to Malaysia.

As I mentioned we had one incidence of race riots in 1969. The damage was minimal compared to Bosnia or Kosovo. But Malaysians were shocked by it. They identified the cause as the disparity in wealth between the Chinese and the indigenous people. A New Economic Policy was adopted designed to redistribute wealth without expropriating the wealth of the rich. Today Malaysia's wealth is more equitably distributed and we have no racial tension anymore. But there has to be eternal vigilance. Given half a chance the extremists will stir up racial feelings and cause tension and riots again.

The Serbs are a very intolerant people. They don't even like the Croats, because they are Catholic. The Serbs are Orthodox Christians. They bombed the Croatian capital, Zagreb. If they were strong enough, if the supporters of Croatia had not warned them they would have conducted ethnic cleansing in Croatia. They wanted to do it even in Slovenia. But certain European countries made it clear from the very beginning that they would not tolerate Serbian attacks against the Slovenes.

In Bosnia-Herzegovina, they killed more than 200,000 people. There were massacres everywhere. In Kosovo, they have killed tens of thousands of ethnic Albanians. The whole world knows that the ethnic Albanians were expelled from their country. Nobody would leave his or her home unless forced to. Nobody wants to live in tents, if they have their houses to live in. If they do it must be because they are forced to.

The Western media often spread untruths but their reporting on Kosovo is not propaganda. NATO's use of force in Yugoslavia is justified. No one should say otherwise unless of course they sanction ethnic cleansing and the mass killing of innocent people.

At the 1991 London Summit, the G-7 countries agreed on the right to use force when a neighbour abuses human rights. This is a radical view as it means that no country can be truly independent. Abuses can occur and have indeed occurred. The fault with this kind of departure from previously accepted norms is that only the weak will be disciplined.

But then, if you are very oppressive, you kill your own people and blatantly abuse human rights, then other countries should intervene to put a stop to it. President Jimmy Carter of the United States was the first to declare that the United States would not respect borders when human rights were abused. President Bush believed in this doctrine when he launched the Gulf War. Because of this stance we see today liberal use of sanctions against countries said to be abusing human rights. Clearly the right to intervene is itself subject to abuses.

In the East, we still believe that we should not interfere in each other's internal affairs because if we do that there will be war. Also, we have very little capacity to do so. Our attitude is different from that of Westerners. But whether we have different attitudes or not, the West still claims that they have the right to interfere in our affairs when they think fit.

This belief in the right to interfere in the internal affairs of countries to stop human right abuses is very frightening for weak nations. This is because one can always claim that a country is abusing human rights. There is no accepted definition as to what constitute human rights and when interference is justified.

There is a vast array of practices in a country's administration and policies which the liberal democrats of powerful countries can define as being against the rights of its people. There are therefore many excuses for the powers that be to interfere in the internal affairs of countries, especially weak countries.

In a unipolar world globalisation and the upholding of human rights have now resulted in the rapid and extensive erosion of the independence of weak nations. It is not what a country does that will attract foreign retribution. It is really who you are. If you are without friends in high places then you will be open to assaults for the slightest mistake made. Even as human rights have many definitions, interference and retribution too can take many forms. In a unipolar world the strong will demand what they will and the weak must yield what they must. Nothing has changed since Thucydides wrote this two thousand years ago.

This is not the end of history as Francis Fukuyama postulated. This is the old story of history repeating itself.

In Southeast Asia we still believe in non-interference in the internal affairs of our neighbours. Unfortunately this resulted in two million Cambodians being killed by the genocidal Khmer Rouge Government. Still this is not something that all Governments which are free from outside interference will always do. Most Governments do care for their people and are seldom unduly harsh even against ethnically different people living in their countries.

Although we do not believe in interference, we do believe in interacting with our neighbours and hoping to influence them. In the ASEAN countries the adoption of the free market system and the willingness to admit foreign direct investments are due to learning from each other's experience. Ultra-nationalistic countries which once rejected foreign involvement in their economy have changed their policies because they see their neighbours benefiting from opening up their countries to foreigners without losing their independence.

We are having a problem at the moment because the European Union refuses to recognise Myanmar as a member of ASEAN. They consider the Government of Myanmar as undemocratic and oppressive. They forget of course that other ASEAN countries had in the past been undemocratic and oppressive and they were happy to sit down with these countries.

It seems to us that the West only understands the use of force. Asians are less aggressive and more patient. We believe that by interacting with Myanmar we would be able to convince them that their people can be accorded increasing degree of freedom. It would take time but it would be less costly than making their people suffer by applying sanctions.

We in Malaysia believe in a 'prosper-thy-neighbour' policy. This is really a self-serving policy. When neighbours are poor or unstable, we will feel the fall out from their situation. Thus when Indochina was poor and unstable we had to receive numerous refugees. They created a problem for us.

By investing in Cambodia and Vietnam, we have contributed a little to their prosperity. As a result there are no more refugees and in addition we are able to trade with them, thus contributing to our economic development. Prospering your neighbour is obviously beneficial for you.

I wish the rich Western countries can understand this. When they invested here and helped build our economy, they benefited not only from their investments but also from being able to sell their products to us because their investments help to make us more prosperous.

Now they have impoverished us through devaluation of our currency and pulling out their short-term capital. As a consequence they have lost a rich market and presumably a lot of profits.

This is what comes from a 'beggar-thy-neighbour' policy. Clearly the West has something to learn from the East. They should discard their pride and learn something from us. Force is not the only way of achieving an objective. It should be resorted to only when everything else fails. Interacting and giving a helping hand can do more at less cost.

CHAPTER 6

LESSONS FROM JAPAN

I MET Japanese Prime Minister Keizo Obuchi when I visited Japan in early June. He is a person who uses his advisers very well. Before giving an opinion or answering a question he would refer to his staff and colleagues first. I believe he knows what he is talking about but is being very careful. A bad leader is somebody who doesn't know and doesn't ask for information or the opinion of others. I am sure that with Mr. Obuchi's leadership and knowledge, Japan can revive its economy.

Revival of the Asian economy is very much dependent on the economic recovery of Japan. It seems that Japan wants to do away with Government/private sector cooperation which has been dubbed "Japan Incorporated" by the West and to replace it quite suddenly with the "so-called" Western concept of separation between Government and the private sector.

Close Government/private sector cooperation was what helped Japan to recover from the wreckage of the Pacific War and go on to become the world's second economic power. Admittedly, there were abuses of the system, but Japan Incorporated worked very well. Dropping it suddenly must cause economic turmoil as people, both from the Government and the private sector, found themselves having to adopt a totally different way of doing work. Matters are agravated by officials and senior members of banks and companies being arrested and charged with doing something that they had always been doing for decades and even centuries. Now neither Government officials nor businessmen dare to do anything which may expose them to legal action and probably jailing. With this atmosphere of uncertainty business cannot succeed.

Admittedly abuses must be got rid off. But this must be done gradually so as to give time for adjustments to be made. If "Japan Incorporated" is to be replaced by other ways of doing business, time must also be given for both the Government officers and businessman to understand and familiarise themselves with the new system. Gradual adoption of the new way of doing business will result in less economic turmoil and disruptions.

It must always be remembered that the Government has a "share" in all businesses in the country. When companies make profit the Government is entitled to a percentage of the profit in the form of corporate tax. If a company fails then the Government will not get to collect the tax.

It is therefore important that the Government ensure that companies do not fail, that in fact they make profits. When a Government under the Japan Incorporated concept helps the companies to make money it is in fact helping itself. Since the Government uses the tax for the good of society, helping the companies to make profits amounts to helping the people. If the Government does not approve of such practices then the Government must accept frequent company failures, low profits and consequently diminished revenue. Economic growth would be stifled and Japan would not have recovered and prospered so quickly after the destruction of its productive capacity due to the war. Abuses are not inevitable.

They can be reduced with proper methods and surveillance. In Malaysia, corporate tax is 28 percent. This actually means that the Government has a 28 percent share in the companies. Clearly we stand to gain by helping the private sector to succeed. But impartiality must be maintained because as far as the Government is concerned, whichever company makes the profit the Government will still get its 28 percent.

A company's failure is a national failure. When a company fails, governments get no money, employees suffer, as do consumers. So you cannot simply allow companies to fail, especially when it is due to no fault on their part, as in a recession.

Because we in Malaysia believe that helping businesses to succeed will help Government revenue to increase, we adopted the Japan Incorporated concept and deliberately propagated what we call Malaysia Incorporated. We regard every businessmen as our crony and we will help them to succeed. When they do, Government revenue is increased, the country's economy grows, people are gainfully employed and the country enjoys a lot of positive spin-off effects.

The devaluation of currencies and plunging share prices will put any company, even the most successful into trouble. They might go bankrupt even. The attacks on the currencies and shares of the East Asian countries had caused many good businesses to fail or to lose money. To recover they need injection of new capital as banks would not lend them money even for normal operation.

Foreign companies and banks of the rich countries thought that they could acquire these businesses and banks cheaply and then inject capital to revive them. This is unwise because the people will resent their companies being taken over by foreigners. In the U.S., foreigners can buy only 24 percent of their airlines. In Canada a company that has always been identified with Canada's history has been taken over 100 percent by Americans. There was a lot of resentment. People cannot avoid feeling that the economy would be controlled by foreigners.

My first overseas holiday was to Hong Kong in 1960 after I left Government service. The next year, I went to Japan. I went to Europe in 1962. I had the opportunity to observe these three peoples. My first impression of Japan was that its post-war recovery was very rapid.

In 1945 Japan lost the war, and the whole country was destroyed. When I went to Japan there were still signs of bomb destruction in various Japanese cities. However, there was also a lot of economic activities.

I went to a factory in Osaka. It was a glass factory, because I use a lot of bottles and thought this was a good business for Malaysia. I also passed the Matsushita factory that was in the middle of a rice field. It looked quite odd to me as factories in Malaysia were not allowed on rice fields. But I could feel that Japan was on the move at that time. Lots of construction was going on. They were preparing for the Olympics, building the highways over Nihonbashi, etc. Of course, everything was cheap at that time.

The trains were always full and I could not get a train ticket back from Osaka to Tokyo. So I had to fly back. I could see that the Japanese people were very determined, focused on working and were very polite to each other. For example, if one car hit another car, both of the drivers came out and bowed to each other. And they seem to settle their problems immediately.

I was also impressed by the train system. The movement of the trains was nonstop and they were very punctual. However, Tokyo was very polluted. There were big factories inside the city giving out a lot of smoke.

As a result of what I observed in Japan, in 1981, after I was appointed Prime Minister of Malaysia, I introduced the "Look East Policy". Because of the race riots in 1969 the country had adopted the New Economic Policy designed to reduce the economic gap between the indigenous Malays and the ethnic Chinese who dominated the business scene.

To make a success of this policy it was necessary to improve the capabilities of the people, the indigenous people in particular. Japan's rapid recovery and growth was due to the character of the Japanese people, their work ethics and their management methods. The Look East policy is not about cutting out the West and giving all contracts to the Japanese. It is about learning Japanese work ethics and business practices. The indigenous people must acquire these ethics and business practices if they were going to make a success of the New Economic Policy. Still it is not possible to change the culture of the people completely, nor is it desirable to do so. But it is easier for the peoples of Malaysia to adopt Japanese ways then to emulate Western ethics and practices.

I have been to Japan more than 50 times and seldom saw signs of poverty. But on my latest trip to Nagoya this year I saw a lot of makeshift huts of the poor people under elevated highways and in parks in the city. I am told that some 6 million people are jobless in Japan. What strikes me is that these people seem to accept their situation.

In other countries, if the unemployment rate goes that high, people will march on the government and protest against its policies. In many cases there would be riots and violence. There was no such reaction in Japan. This self-restrain is remarkable. Riots and violence can only worsen the situation and make the cost of recovery higher. I was told that these people chose to escape from their families rather than be a burden to them. Since they did not register as being unemployed they did not get Government aid. They have to eke out a living by collecting discarded things and selling them. I don't think that this is good. In Malaysia we have no unemployment benefit. We expect families to look after their unemployed members. Not wanting to be a burden to their families these unemployed people would try to get employment as soon as possible.

Still the Japanese are nationalistic and proud of their independence and skills. However over the past five years or so, the Japanese seem to have lost some of their self-confidence and even national pride. It is right not to be militaristic but it is not wrong to be nationalistic. Nationalism motivates and helps a country to overcome problems. Alliances with other countries should not result in total dependence. To be able to defend one's own country is not synonymous with aggressive militarism.

Japan has a good reason for rejecting militarism. It should be ready and willing to admit that it had done a lot of wrong in the past. But it should not be burdened by a permanent sense of guilt over actions committed more than half a century ago. I don't see Germany being reminded of its Nazi past. Nor is Germany required to go around apologising for Nazi atrocities during the war. But it would seem that every Japanese Prime Minister must apologise for deeds committed by people of two generations ago. Apologies are not needed but undertaking not to be an aggressive military power is necessary if Japan wants to allay the fears of its neighbours.

The Self-Defense Force is necessary but it must not limit itself to internal duties only. While it should not attack other countries, it should be prepared to help the peace-keeping functions of the United Nations.

Japan feels a need to be allied to the United States. This is understandable if it is not directed at other nations. Unfortunately the U.S. shows open hostility to some countries in Asia and the U.S.-Japan alliance seems to be directed against these countries. This is not good because these countries would regard Japan as an enemy and there would always be tension in the region.

Malaysia does not want to have any enemy. That is why we say we are against the presence of foreign forces in the region. War is no longer a way of solving international problems. If there is another world war, the whole world would be destroyed.

I believe that nuclear weapons should be abolished, although physically that is going to be very difficult if not impossible. No one knows what to do with nuclear warheads. But even so-called conventional weapons are getting more and more sophisticated and expensive. A lot of money is now spent in periodical testing of new weapons. There should be international agreement to reduce research on new weapons. Then poor countries need not spend so much money in acquiring new weapons to match the new ones acquired by neighbours. But unfortunately some countries refuse even to outlaw land mines. Why land mines should seem so necessary when missiles can reach any point on earth is something I cannot understand.

As much as Japan fears China, China must fear the U.S. - Japan alliance. However the world must accept that China, with 1.3 billion very hard working, intelligent people cannot help but be a powerful country eventually. We have to live with this eventuality. If we can live with the U.S. as the sole superpower, there is no reason why we cannot live with China as a world power. China has practically no history of conquering and colonising neighbours. European powers have.

I believe that all conflicts should be resolved around the table. That is why we should support the East Asia Economic Caucus. Through the caucus we can resolve problems between us and discuss common problems facing the region. Europe has the European Union and North America has NAFTA. We accept them. Why cannot they accept the East Asia Economic Caucus. Japan should rethink the EAEC. It should not be led into believing that it is going to be a threat to countries outside the region.

East Asia needs the economic and financial strength of Japan. We welcomed Japan's 1997 proposal for a USD 100 billion Asian Monetary Fund. Unfortunately Japan dropped the proposal due to U.S. opposition. Later the Japanese government introduced the 30-billion dollar Miyazawa Plan. This has been very helpful for Asia's recovery. A newspaper reported that there was some opposition to the fund being made available to Malaysia. Fortunately the Japanese Government stood firm and provided loan to Malaysia. I hope that the Japanese will always stand by its friends in times of need regardless of pressures from elsewhere. Asians prosperity will help Japan to recover. In helping Asia, Japan will also be helping itself.

CHAPTER 7

THE CURRENCY CONTROL

IT IS NOW almost a year since Malaysia introduced selective capital control. Initially we were worried over whether or not the control would work. The criticisms levelled at us by the international press and foreign financial experts did not help to strengthen our confidence in the measures that we took to revive our economy. But our doubts soon disappeared as almost immediately we saw signs of economic recovery.

Currency control as imposed by Malaysia is not generally understood by the international financial community. Their criticisms are therefore based more on their text-book models than on proper examination of what Malaysia has done. To understand the measures we took it is necessary to look at the root cause of the financial turmoil which undermined the economy of the country.

The Malaysian economy and finances were very sound prior to the July 1997 attack on the Ringgit. We had good reserves and very little foreign debts either by the Government or the private sector. There really was no reason why the currency should become weak.

But the currency traders in their quest for big profits borrowed the Ringgit and sold it down repeatedly, thus devaluing it almost by 100 percent. This meant our wealth was halved in terms of purchasing imported goods. Inflation set in and people found difficulty in making ends meet.

To make matters worse the foreign investors in the stock market began to dump their shares and to short-sell. They did this through the Singapore operated Central Limit Order Book (CLOB) which traded in Malaysian shares without the approval of the Kuala Lumpur Stock Exchange (KLSE) or the Malaysian Government. By registering all shares held by thousands of investors under the name of a few nominee companies, trading through CLOB did not require registration with the KLSE. The nominee companies were able to lend the shares to speculators who short-sell them and caused the prices to plunge. Through CLOB the Composite Index of the KLSE went down from 1200 to 260 points.

Between the depreciation of the Ringgit and the severe fall in share prices, the companies and the banks rapidly deteriorated and were bankrupted or became nearly so. The Government too faced revenue shortfalls as businesses were unable to make any profit and could pay no tax.

Clearly the country's economy would collapse completely if the currency continued to depreciate and the share prices remain very low. To prevent this it was imperative for the Government ro regain control of the exchange rate of the Ringgit and to stop CLOB from destroying the Malaysian share market any further.

To devalue the Ringgit the traders had to borrow and sell it. Singapore offered high interest rates so as to lure the Ringgit to Singapore where it was lent to the currency traders. The Malaysian banks found themselves without money to lend. To stop this outflow of the currency the Government decreed that if within one month the offshore Ringgit in whatever form is not repatriated to Malaysia it will not be allowed to be brought back at all. Effectively this rendered offshore Ringgits worthless after one month.

This forced all offshore Ringgits to be repatriated within one month leaving nothing for the traders to borrow and manipulate. Trading in Ringgit ceased and the Government was able to fix and stabilise the exchange rate at RM3.80 to one US Dollar.

As for CLOB and the short-selling activities; this was stopped by abolishing the right of nominee companies to hold the shares of their clients. Since all sales of shares must be registered with the KLSE in the name of the share holders and sales outside the KLSE are not recognised, the business of CLOB stopped. Short-selling of borrowed shares held by the nominee companies could no longer be done and manipulation of share prices ceased.

The net result was stability of exchange rates and a rise in share prices on the KLSE. The forced repatriation of funds from Singapore resulted in more money being available for loans. It was therefore possible to lower the interest rates to stimulate consumption and business activities.

Many other measures were taken such as setting up an Asset Management Company to deal with Non-Performing Loans and the recapitalisation of banks through a Recapitalisation Fund. Every aspect of the economy was studied by a National Economic Action Council (NEAC) set up to take counter measures if the economy is faced with any problem. For example imports of non-essentials were reduced while exports were encouraged. The balance of payment which had been in deficit for many years was reversed and huge surpluses achieved in the trade balance. This enabled the reserves to increase from USD20 billion to USD30 billion in the space of 6 months.

All other indicators show that the economy is improving rapidly and it is expected that the target of one percent growth of the GDP for 1999 will be achieved easily. It is expected that the growth in year 2000 will be around 5 percent.

The controls have apparently succeeded in bringing about the recovery of the Malaysian economy. Although many still condemn capital controls others now say that controls can resolve the problems brought about by the rapid devaluation of the currency by currency traders. Some even recommend that other countries open to attacks by currency speculators should adopt currency controls.

It is now easy to think that countries should at least try currency controls in order to solve the problem created by currency devaluation by unscrupulous traders. But deciding on such controls is not easy. In the case of Malaysia, more than 6 months of intense debate preceded the decision by the executive committee of the NEAC to impose controls. One member of the executive committee brought up 32 reasons why currency controls would be bad for the country; would fail. But the arguments were demolished one by one.

Other members of the NEAC Exco also found difficulty in supporting the proposal. The Deputy Governor of the Central Bank was invited to give his opinion and he too was not supportive. He gave all the standard reasons why it would harm the country, its economy and its relations with the rest of the world.

The former Deputy Prime Minister was still a member of the NEAC Executive all the time the controls were being discussed. Although he had favoured and implemented all the IMF solutions for dealing with the country's deteriorating economy and finances during the turmoil he did not argue against the controls. When the decision was finally made to impose the controls he agreed with the decision. It was decided that September 1st was the date for the controls to be implemented. There is no particular reason for choosing this date except that we reached agreement in August 1998 and wanted to implement control as soon as possible.

But when the date was almost due, the Governor of the Central Bank and his deputy tried to scuttle it by resigning.

This was a heavy blow as the Central Bank was the principal implementing authority under the law. Immediately the most senior officer of the Central Bank was given the responsibility for carrying out the various actions to make the Malaysian Ringgit invalid outside the country and to require all shareholders of Malaysian companies to register their ownership directly with the Malaysian Stock Exchange, thus eliminating the nominee companies.

Currency controls mean different things to different people. To the text-book economists currency control means cutting the country off from every kind of financial links with the rest of the world. The Malaysian control is not a simple turning your back to the world. Malaysia is a trading nation. Its economic growth and well-being depends largely on its commercial and financial links, including direct foreign investments with the rest of the world. It is not like the United States which can actually cut itself off from the rest of the world and still survive and even prosper. With only 22 million people and a relatively low per capita income there is no way for Malaysia to be totally independent economically and certainly no way for Malaysia to grow and prosper. Malaysia must maintain strong economic links with the rest of the world.

And so Malaysian currency control had to be so crafted that it would prevent the currency from being manipulated by foreign currency traders while allowing normal business transactions to be carried out without hindrance. And that is precisely what was formulated and carried out.

Trade has therefore not been in any way affected and it has not only grown much bigger but the surplus has increased considerably. The foreign currency to pay for imports is thus readily available from the surplus.

Foreign long-term direct investments has not been affected either. The investments are flowing in because conversion to Ringgit at a fixed rate within the country facilitates business budgeting. At the same time the exchange rate is more favourable than when the Ringgit was stronger. The money invested can be taken out without any difficulty if there is a need to liquidate and take the money in foreign currency elsewhere. Profits from such long-term investments can be repatriated.

Clearly the movement of foreign funds in and out of the country is not affected by our selective currency control. However short-term investments in the stock-market is subject to some tolerable conditions. The capital must stay in the country for at least a year and earlier repatriation would be subjected to an exit tax. Apparently these conditions have not stopped foreign short-term investors from coming in.

Today Malaysia's economy is growing again. We believe it is due to the controls we have imposed. But our detractors disagree and point out that the economies of other East Asian countries are also recovering. They say that even without controls Malaysia would recover.

We believe that the recovery of other East Asian economies is due to the currency traders stopping their manipulation of the currencies. There are several reasons why they stopped. When Malaysia imposed controls there was a fear that the other countries might do the same if the attacks continued. Secondly at about this time the Long Term Capital Management Fund collapsed threatening to destablise the financial system of the rich countries. As a result the banks stopped lending to the hedge funds, thus stopping them from attacking and devaluing the currencies of East Asia.

Freed of the threat posed by the currency traders the countries were able to ignore the IMF prescription for countering currency devaluation. They lowered their interest rates and expanded their budgets. The big conglomerates which had been ordered to dismantle did not really do so.

And so the economies of South Korea and Thailand recovered. Even the Indonesian Rupiah strengthened. But

Malaysia's recovery is earlier and stronger. The business community both local and foreign are convinced that controls have benefited them. The investing public returned to the stock exchange and help push up the Composite Index by almost 200 percent. With this the companies were freed from the need to meet margin calls by their banks and were able to do business again. The Reserve of the Central Bank shot up by 50 percent as the trade surpluses increased. All other indices indicate a positive recovery for the Malaysian economy.

Malaysia's currency control is made possible by its strong economic fundamentals. The Reserves stood at USD20 billion when controls were imposed. There was hardly any foreign debt. The financial system and the bankruptcy laws were already in place. The political climate was stable and the Government was backed by a big majority. Inflation was low even when the currency was devalued. Reduction in imports and expanding exports had resulted in huge surpluses.

The initial attempt to raise funds through bond issues was frustrated by Moody's and Standard and Poor's downrating Malaysia's credit rating to almost junk bond level. But the high savings rates of almost 40 percent and the repatriation of the Ringgit from abroad enabled Malaysia to ignore the failure to raise funds from abroad. There was sufficient funds within the system.

At this stage Japan came to the rescue by making available substantial soft loans amounting to several billion US dollars. Japan was also prepared to guarantee any bond issue by the Malaysian Government. And so despite Moody's and Standard and Poor's low ratings, when the Government tested the American bond market in 1999, the issue was oversubscribed by three times.

The country is now in a sound financial position. The economy is growing and many predict that it will exceed the one percent GDP growth estimated by the Government.

The Ringgit is still pegged at RM3.80 to one US Dollar even though the currencies of the neighbouring countries have strengthen further against the Dollar and therefore against the Ringgit. We do not want to change the exchange rate because this will upset the business transactions and profit forecasts. Besides a weak Ringgit makes us more competitive even if the cost of imports is higher. This high cost of import can result in inflation of course. But Malaysia has always had low inflation rates. We counter imported inflation by producing more for domestic consumption. Since the food import is the biggest item contributing to our high cost, we have encouraged local food production. This has been so successful that we can now export more food products, thus increasing our trade surplus.

With the Government in full control of the exchange rate we can easily enrich ourselves by strengthening the Ringgit, even up to the pre-turmoil level of RM2.50 to the US dollar. But the downside to this is lesser competitiveness of our exports and therefore less foreign and domestic investments for export industries. The power to change exchange rates must be used judiciously or the economy would be damaged.

The recovery of the East Asian economies also owe a lot to the Chinese Government's decision not to devalue the Yuan. Had the Yuan been freely convertible there is no doubt that the currency traders would have attacked it and plunged China and East Asia in even worse turmoil and recession. As it is they tried to attack Hong Kong instead in an effort to destabilise China. The Hong Kong Government departed from its laissez faire policy and defended the stock market strongly. The attack failed but Hong Kong's economy and its reputation has been damaged.

It is really not fair to expect China not to devalue the Yuan forever. The devaluation of the currencies of East Asia has effectively revalued upwards the Yuan, rendering China less competitive. The Yuan can actually be devalued a little without affecting the economies of the East Asian countries. But I must thank the Chinese Government for holding steadfastly to its promise not to devalue the Yuan. China is a friend indeed, much more so than some other so-called friends.

As I mentioned the former Deputy Prime Minister was still in the Government when the decision was made to control exchange rate and short term capital flows. He did not object to the decision in any way. So economic reasons are not involved in his removal from office.

He was removed purely for behaviour which are not acceptable in a member of the Government. It was certainly not a good time to remove him. We were about to defy the world with a strategy that we could not be certain would work. We were in a state of recession and severe economic turmoil. No one in his right mind would want to add political instability to the already difficult economic situation. If the removal of the Deputy Prime Minister was planned a more propituous time would have been found. But his misbehaviour was such that his immediate removal was necessary. And so a political problem was added to the economic problem for the Government to tackle.

Upon dismissal the former Deputy Prime Minister was allowed to move around the country freely to hold rallies to whip up anti-Government feelings. The Government did not stop him. This apparently did not suit his purpose. He wanted to convince his followers and foreign observers that the Malaysian Government and in particular the Prime Minister is dictatorial and violently oppressive. And so he organised demonstrations and rioting by his followers in Kuala Lumpur. The Government was forced to arrest and detain him. With that his followers became truly incensed and violent. They started to domonstrate and to riot in Kuala Lumpur.

The foreign press seized on this to depict Malaysia as an undemocratic, unstable, potentially violent country. Day in and day out pictures of rioting were shown by CNN, CNBC, BBC and others. This compounded the difficulties in reviving the economy. Investors and tourists avoided the country and the hotels and other service industries suffered very badly.

But the demonstration and riots pettered out and try as they might the dectractors could not keep up with the picture that Malaysia is a bad country. When the ex-Deputy Prime Minister was found guilty after a much prolonged trial witnessed by foreign and local journalists, diplomats and sundry NGOs, there was another bout of rioting, but it did not last. Today the Anwar affair is no longer relevant as far as the economic recovery is concerned.

In the meantime the economy is growing again. More and more experts are supporting currency control, condemning the IMF and even indirectly the powerful and influential hedge funds and currency traders. Even the G-7 is discussing regulating the activities of the hedge funds. It will be a long time before they will actually do something but at least they recognise the role of the currency traders in causing the worldwide economic turmoil. If they do it again, the funds will certainly be dealt with appropriately.

The question that has been asked repeatedly is when will the controls be lifted. Many say that the objectives have been achieved and Malaysia should go back to the freely convertible currency. The Ringgit should be allowed to cross the border freely.

We have said right from the beginning that the present international financial regime exposes newly emerging economies and middle income countries to very destructive currency trading and manipulation by the hedge funds and other currency traders. The only way this danger can be eliminated is by curbing the activities of these traders, by regulating currency trading, by making them accountable and transparent. All these things can be done if the powerful economies of the world will agree to do so and to assert their authority over their own nationals. We have seen how a super-power can actually ignore international norms and arrest the leader of a foreign country to bring him for trial under the laws of the superpower. If this can be done I don't see why currency traders who have in fact destroyed the economies of whole regions of the world, precipitating riots, looting and killing, cannot be curbed and their activities regulated. Free trade is not a religion that anything done in its name cannot be modified, regulated or banned altogether.

If and when currency trading is rendered less harmful to emerging economies Malaysia will lift its selective capital cont-rol. Until then the controls will remain in place and will be defended and kept effective by whatever means that Malaysia has at its disposal. We are doing nobody any harm by our controls. Indeed we are doing a lot of good to ourselves and I venture to say, to our trading partners, investors and even the world's economy. So I hope we will be left to administer our economy in our own way. No one should tell us when we should lift the controls.

On Sept 1st 1999 we will celebrate one year of defying con-vention. We would of course make an assessment of the results. We think it is going to be good. Some will take the money they have invested in our share market out. That is alright. We will change their Ringgit into whatever currency they wish so they can take it out. We will not bear any ill-feelings towards them. That is their right and in Malaysia we respect the rights of everyone including foreigners.

We are prepared to face challenges and we believe we can handle most of them. Whether we fail or succeed we hope we have provided the world with an experience which will be use-ful for case studies in the management of a country's economy under stress.

CHAPTER 8

MY VISIT TO CHINA

I WENT to China in August for ceremonies marking the 25th anniversary of the establishment of diplomatic ties between Malaysia and China. The occasion gave me a chance to meet with Chinese President Jiang Zemin and Prime Minister Zhu Rongji.

During our discussions, Prime Minister Zhu assured me that his country would not devalue the Yuan. I responded by saying that even if China were to devalue a little, it would not hurt the Malaysian or other East Asian economy. We have already devalued so much that even if the Yuan is devalued by 10 percent, our economy will stay on course.

Zhu assured me that China would stick by the Yuan because the economy is performing well and is still growing. The restructuring of state enterprises has at times proved difficult as it tends to be disruptive for the workers employed in those industries.

Nonetheless, Zhu expressed confidence that the problems associated with restructuring could be solved.

My talks with President Jiang, on the other hand, leaned toward political issues. Jiang indicated that he was very unhappy with the attitude of Taiwan about its position vis-a-vis mainland China and warned against support for those seeking to create two separate Chinese states.

As far as Malaysia is concerned, we still subscribe to our One China policy. We will not alter that policy because it helps stabililize the region. We cannot afford to have two Chinas. Such a situation would create a lot of conflict. China will not tolerate it, and China is a close friend of Malaysia, as well as major trading partner.

However, my country also has business ties with Taiwan and we have a business representative in Taipei. Likewise, Taiwan maintains a representative office in Malaysia to facilitiate business contacts and issue travel documents.

In my opinion, President Lee Teng-hui's suggestion that contacts across the Taiwan Straits be conducted at the state-to-state level is really not realistic. No major country will recognize Taiwan as a state.

It is a futile effort that doesn't bring anything in the way of benefits to anyone. Taiwan should remain in the same position as it is now. They lose nothing by doing so. Provocation, on the other, could have very negative consequences. Taiwan should accept the formula that applies to Hong Kong since it reverted to Chinese rule: One country, two systems.

Jiang also mentioned his unhappiness over the NATO bombing of the Chinese Embassy in Belgrade, Yugoslavia, during the conflict over Kosovo. He said China was unhappy with NATO's action against the Serbs, but added that his country did not say anything nor interfere.

However, public outrage at the NATO action grew in the wake of the bombing and strained the relation between the United States and China. I don't see how NATO could attribute the incident to incorrect information about the location of the Chinese Embassy. It was there for a long time, and everybody knew where the Chinese embassy was.

The United States possesses very sophisticated bombs that

are able to hit targets with deadly accuracy. It is impossible to imagine them making such a gross mistake.

Furthermore, Jiang expressed unhappiness about the U.S. actions to block China's entry into the World Trade Organization (WTO). Washington has set all sorts of conditions for China's accession to the world body. China is a big nation with a huge market. If China is to open up its huge market to the world then the world must open up to China. It is only fair to expect this. There must be reciprocity. Nontrade issues should not be brought in to frustrate China.

The U.S. position of putting conditions on China's entry to the world body is not right. Whether to admit China or not should be the decision of WTO, not that of the United States alone. I can well understand China's desire as a developing country to join the WTO. Malaysia supports its admission to the WTO, as do the majority of the member countries of the WTO.

We subscribe to the World Trade Organisation as an international body. Matters affecting world trade should be decided by the WTO as a whole. No one, however powerful should arrogate to itself the right to determine WTO policy. If this is done than the WTO would no longer be an international organisation. If it is not an international organisation no one would willingly join it.

The United States always brings up the issue of human rights in China. China may have violated some human rights, but other countries are just as guilty. If you define human rights not just as political rights or the right against oppression by the Government, but include such things as the right to live our own way of life, the right to work, to earn a living, then we will see how Western countries had deprived millions of people in East Asia and elsewhere of their rights. The attacks against the currencies of these countries have thrown millions out of work, deprived them of food, medicine and milk for their children. The riots which followed resulted in looting, raping and killing of innocent people. This is a greater abuse of human rights than the action taken by China against a few of its 1.2 billion citizens.

Then of course there is the sanctions and daily bombings of Iraq. Many innocent Iraqi civilians have been wounded and killed, thousands have no food or medicine and many children and new-born babies died as a result. Aren't these things worse abuses of human rights than what is perpetrated by China? Too much emphasis and attention has been given to the right of political dissent that other major abuses of human rights are allowed to go on uncensured. The NGOs, a creation of the West, seem unable to notice these blatant violations, while they agitate against lesser violations.

There may indeed be cases of human rights violations in China, but there is also the matter of 1.2 billion people whose rights have been denied because China is not able to become a member of the WTO.

The United States should not always find faults with China and treat it as an enemy or potential enemy. The United States should regard China as a major trade partner which can lower the cost of living for the U.S. and other countries.

While I was visiting China, the Chinese government banned the Falun Gong sect. I think it is natural that a government should worry when a movement such as Falun Gong becomes too big and too powerful, as it is bound to try to impose its will on the government and the rest of the people. So the government was wise to take steps to ensure that such movements don't create problems for the country and the government. This is an internal affair of China. The Western world cannot always make use of trade and media campaigns to force other countries to submit to the Western way of thinking and doing things.

I know President Jiang quite well. He is a man who wants to bring China into the mainstream and has long been responsible for promoting direct foreign investment in China and setting up free-trade zones. That prompted him to come to Malaysia a long time ago to study our free-trade zone. He is very concerned about his country, which he wants to develop. He is keen to have good relations with other countries. including Malaysia. What's more, he is easy to talk with.

I have met Premier Zhu for two or three times. He is a very knowledgeable man and can discuss Sino-Malaysian relations in detail, including such business-oriented matters as our intention to sell liquified natural gas to China. He is well able to run the government, in particular economic matters.

I didn't see much difference in the views of the two men, though Zhu tends to focus more on economic matters and Jiang focuses on political matters. I thought they get along very well. A stable China is good for us.

China is a country with great potential, and it has 1.2 billion hard-working, intelligent and skilled people. We cannot keep China down forever. Whatever we do, China is going to develop and will grow. It may not became as prosperous as the United States because of its huge population, but even the small per capita income will add up to very large GDP. Because China will become a powerful economy, it will have considerable influence over the world. That is something that we must accept. Trying to stop China from developing is counter productive. It will only make us seem like enemies.

When they did not devalue the Yuan, it helped us in Southeast Asia. We didn't have to compete with cheap Chinese products. If China had devalued then the currency traders would have a great time devaluing the currencies of East Asian countries further and reaping huge profits. The economic problems of East Asia would worsen while the rich Western countries would enjoy low inflation as they import very cheap East Asian products. Economic recovery for East Asia would take a long time to achieve. Even then there would not be full recovery.

I think Japan should have a balanced view of its relationship with China and the United States. Japan should not always follow the United States. The Japanese commitment to the Guidelines for Japan U.S. Defense Cooperation is obviously directed at China. China cannot be blamed if it too prepares against an open alliance directed at it. An arms race must follow and this will only exacerbate tensions. I think there should be less talk of military alliances. I don't think war is a solution nowadays. It was never a solution in the past. Now, if two nuclear powers go to war, peaceful countries are not going to be spared. The war will be total.

My trip to China was very educational. I met the leaders and learned first-hand their views. They are pragmatic people, who are concerned about their citizens. I also got to see the development of China. Many of the country's cities are better provided with infrastructure. Dalian for example is a city that has been landscaped and beautified with lots of flowers.

In order to do that, you must have a good economy. The China leaders, lead by Deng Xiao Ping may believe that being rich is glorious. But they are more cautious in their approach towards getting rich. While they acknowledge the need to switch from their authoritarian style of Government and to do away with the command economy, they did not rush things. Economic reforms towards a free market was carried out gradually. They kept much of their system of Government because they know only a strong Government can carry out the kind of reforms they had to undertake.

As a result China fared better than the other Communist command economies which tried to switch both the political system and the economic creed overnight. The democratic Governments they set up lacked experience and competence and could not function properly. On the other hand after 70 years of Communism they had no entrepreneurs, managers or private capital to make a success of the free market economy. They failed miserably or succeeded only at considerable cost in terms of disruptions and human sufferings.

The Chinese refusal to swallow Liberal democracy and the market economy at one go, but with circumspection and care instead, saved China from disaster and possible rebellion and blooshed. The economy has grown while more moderation is seen in the Government. Others may chafe because China has not embraced democracy fully, but if democracy will only lead to violence and the death of millions; it is better that the espousal of democracy be more gradual. It is important to remember that it is not the system which is important; it is the results that count. The well-being of the vast majority of China's 1.2 billion people is more important than the right of dissent for a very few.

While in Beijing I spoke at The 3rd Malaysia-China Forum. I once again raised the need to set up the East Asia Economic Caucus. I felt sure that had the caucus been in place, much could have been done to protect the East Asian countries from the assault by currency traders on their economies. Certainly they would have been able to exchange information and to devise strategies to save their economies. The Japanese idea of an Asian Monetary Fund would have been fully discussed and suggestions could be made to realise it and to work out its uses and applications. Much could have been saved not just for the East Asian economies but for the world's economy as well if the East Asian Caucus had been in place.

It seems grossly unfair that while Europe can form the European Union and the US, Canada and Mexico can form NAFTA, and even the Latin American countries can form their regional organisations, East Asia is not allowed to do so. If one does not know better one would be tempted to believe that the opposition to it is racial.

It would seem that Asian countries cannot form their own grouping without the supervising presence of the U.S., Australia and New Zealand. Already APEC which includes the U.S. has come to dominate the East Asian economy. Yet

APEC is either unwilling or powerless to help the East Asian countries during the economic and financial turmoil. Instead it passed the buck to a lesser organisation, the Group of 22. APEC is now focussed only on prising open the Asian markets as early as possible. And we know who will gain from this.

We talk a lot about individual freedom. When countries and regions are not allowed their freedom, then millions of individuals who chose their Governments effectively lose their freedom as well. The loss is real for the decisions of their Governments impinges on them directly and personally. Thus when East Asia was attacked by the currency traders, individuals, as workers, traders and businessmen lose their freedom and actually and truly suffer. There cannot be individual human rights if there are no rights for free nations.

China supports the EAEC and reaffirms their commitment. But of course without the support of Japan and South Korea, the EAEC cannot become a reality. It is a pity because the EAEC can be a force for the good not only of East Asia but also the world.

The trip to China was short but it was an eventful one for me. It served the cause of good neighbourliness and it revealed China's ability to weather the storm of the East Asian turmoil and to continue to develop itself.

Despite everything China is making tremendous progress. It is still autocratic of course, but governing 1.2 billion people as energetic as the Chinese is not the easiest thing in the world. Democracy can only come when people understand its limitations and their responsibilities. When the Chinese people as a whole are better able to understand this, democracy will come to China.

CHAPTER 9

MY THOUGHTS
ON EAST TIMOR

THE EAST TIMOR issue has been very badly handled. The East Timorese were generally not happy being included as a part of Indonesia. But there are many East Timorese people who have become reconciled with integration. The West has always rejected Indonesia's occupation of East Timor, although the West had in the past closed its eyes to similar occupation by other countries. If they wanted the East Timorese to have independence, they could have handled it in a much more diplomatic way, to avoid the bloodshed and the bitterness of Indonesia against the East Timorese which will make their relations very difficult in the future.

It is clear that the West wanted to frustrate Indonesia at any cost. But since they regarded Indonesia as a close ally and a strong one at that, they did not really exert pressure on Indonesia in the past. In fact Australia went so far as to acknowledge the de facto integration of East Timor into Indonesia. It entered into an agreement with Indonesia to recognise the sea boundary which gave Indonesia much of the potentially oil-rich continental shelf and economic zone between the island of Timor and Northern Australia. It developed a very close relation with Indonesia and provided military training for the armed forces.

The big Western powers did not openly object to Australia's separate stand on the question of East Timor. Over time it is likely that the Indonesian annexation of East Timor would have been recognised.

It should be remembered that although the East Timorese are Christians, there are many Indonesians who are Christians. They apparently lived in harmony with the majority Muslim population. East Timorese Christians would have little difficulty in doing the same.

But then the currency traders devalued the Indonesian Rupiah by 600 percent, reducing this Asian Tiger into a basket case. Indonesia was rocked by race riots, student demonstrations and violent political agitation which forced it not only to seek IMF loans but to surrender direction over its economy as well. With control of the economy in foreign hands Indonesia was forced to submit to political direction as well. An Army-backed virtual autocracy was changed overnight into a democracy with unlimited freedom of political action. The subsequent race for power deeply divided the Indonesian people into numerous political parties, none of which are strong enough to rule the vast 13,000 island archipelago of 220 million tribally distinct people.

It is well-known that the West would like to see Indonesia broken up into smaller countries. Early during the Sukarno period rebels in Sumatra and Sulawesi were actually supplied with arms and foreign pilots flew bombing missions in their support. But the Indonesians supported Sukarno and a unified Indonesia. Although that attempt failed the desire to see Indonesia fragmented and weaken is clearly still there.

And so when the currency crisis plunged Indonesia into political and economic turmoil and Suharto was overthrown, the West seized the opportunity to once again break up Indonesia. This time the focus is on East Timor, Irian Jaya,

Acheh and Sulawesi where there are rumblings against the Central Government. East Timor presented the best possibility for this new attempt. The Australians, never very sincere in its support of Indonesian annexation, quickly changed its stance and became the most bitter opponent of Indonesian action.

With the Government weakened and the military unable to restore law and order due to the ever present foreign video cameras (In Western countries if a policeman beats or shoots a rioter to death, the policeman is blamed but the Government is considered innocent. In non-Western countries if the police so much as hurt a violent, stone throwing, car burning rioter, it is assumed that the Government had instructed the police to do so. With this effective law enforcement becomes quite impossible), the Western countries exerted pressure on the Government to part with Timor-Timor.

Indonesians may disagree on who should govern the country but they are united over keeping Indonesia and Indonesian possessions intact. The decision of the Indonesian Government to hold a referendum in Timor-Timur was unpopular except with those convinced that the majority of the Timorese would vote for integration.

It is very probable that given a free choice the Timorese would opt for independence. But the West made sure that the Timorese voted for independence through overt propaganda, support, promises of protection and aid for independent Timor. The Indonesian's hope was smashed as the Timorese voted overwhelmingly for independence. While the Government may want to be reasonable and to accept the result, the ordinary Indonesian, the settlers in particular are not prepared to face this humiliation. And so violence erupted.

East Timor's separation from Indonesia may not represent much in terms of breaking up the country. But there are other parts of Indonesia which seem to be ripe for breaking off. Media propaganda will be mounted and more and more pressure will be brought to bear on Indonesia especially if the Government is weak. Indonesian blood will be spilt but this of course is not a concern of the West.

The main beneficiary of a broken up Indonesia will be Australia. It is not surprising that Australian forces have moved into Timor-Timor first. The need to protect Timor-Timor will be permanent and Australia is ready to provide this protection. It may become Australia's Vietnam.

Already Australia is talking about becoming the deputy to the United States in policing Asia. This is unmitigated arrogance. But then when Australians claim to be Asian, they only see themselves as lording it over Asia. Asians realise this and that is why they did not welcome Australia into the proposed East Asia Economic Caucus. To ensure that Australia - less EAEC is not formed, Australia enlisted the United States to make APEC the principle organisation in East Asia; at one stroke spiking the EAEC and the ASEAN as well. Today ASEAN is split up and unable to do much to counter the campaign to break up Indonesia as well as the onslaught against the economies of Southeast Asia.

If the East Timor issue is being badly handled, how should it have been better handled. In the first place Indonesia should not have been forced to make a decision on East Timor at the time when it is trying to cope with liberal democracy. We have seen many countries trying to switch to liberal democracy making a mess of things. It was not the best of times for making decisions. Indonesia should have been allowed to adapt to democracy fully before being called upon to decide on East Timor. It is of course likely that a truly democratic Indonesia would make the East Timorese decide in favour of integration. Even if they don't the separation would not be so bloody.

Asian problems or at least East Asian problems should be

resolved by Asians in the Asian way. Historically Asians did not practise the policy of divide and rule nor did Asians colonise territories in order to exploit the local inhabitants. If Asians conquer territories, as the Mongols did, the conquerors tended to be absorbed by the locals. Thus in West and Central Asia they were absorbed by Turkic people and became Muslims, in Northern India the Moguls (Mongol) were also Muslim while in China they became Buddhist Chinese.

Asian powers never protect their citizens living in other lands by sending a punitive force. When Asians lose people in a war they never make a permanent issue of it, never demanded that the bodies be returned or diplomatic relations would not be possible.

Asians compete by making sacrifices. They would eat poor quality rice in order to export good rice. They would pay their workers low wages in order to keep their costs down. Asians would not insist that others do what they do in order to retain the competitiveness of Asians.

Had the Asians been left to themselves there would not be a financial and economic turmoil in Asia. Asian currency traders did not initiate the trading which devalued Asian currencies and impoverished the whole of Southeast Asia. There would not have been the destabilisation of Indonesia and the overthrow of the Suharto Government. East Timor would have progressed towards eventual full integration.

Is the integration of East Timor so bad that it must be stopped at any cost. Indonesia had poured a lot of money into the development of East Timor, more than the Portuguese did in 400 years. A lot of East Timorese had already become reconciled with the idea of being a part of Indonesia. There was a chance that East Timor would be peaceful and much better off than when it was a Portuguese colony.

The Asians would have accepted this. But not so the Europeans. They encouraged East Timor intransigence, they gave the Nobel Prize to separatists, they did everything possi-

ble to keep alive the hatred for Indonesia among the Timorese.
For as long as the West is able to meddle in the affairs of
East Asia, there will always be tensions and confrontations
between the countries of the region. If East Asia wants to have
peace, to develop and to take its rightful place in the world,
the East Asian Nations must come together to discuss and
resolve mutual problems in an amicable way and to help each
other in time of need.

We should leave the baggage of history behind us. The
Pacific war ended 50 years ago. In Europe Germany is completely accepted as a peaceful democracy. Its military forces
are big and sophisticated because there is no restriction on its
rearming. Its leaders are not required to go around apologising for the crimes of the Nazis in the past, not even to Israel
or the Jewish world, We in East Asia should be prepared to
forget the past and concentrate on the present and the future.

The globalised borderless world is largely the invention of
the West. Quite naturally the present interpretation of this
brave new world benefit the West mostly. We have seen what
the free flow capital can do to our economies. Even wealthy
Japan can be made poor if the Yen rises to 50 to the dollar and
Japan as a believer in non-interference by the Government in
the market refuses to weaken the Yen. Japan's commitment to
the principle of free convertibility would be questioned if it
tries to impose the kind of selective capital control as Malaysia
has done.

A few countries have talked about linking to the Yen.
Imagine what would happen to their export if they had done
so. They would be absolutely uncompetitive. They would not
attract foreign investments. Their economies would collapse.
If all of East Asia is linked to the Yen then all of East Asia
would collapse.

It is not only devaluation which can destroy economies but
revaluation can do the same. Yet we think we must uphold
our commitment to the free convertibility of our currency

because we have given our word of honour and we will keep our commitment even if it kills us and all our friends together.

East Asian countries must realise that they have as much right to interpret the meaning of globalisation as the West. We should not be afraid to challenge current accepted wisdom. In the history of the world so many things believed to be right and just have been found otherwise and have been discarded. Asians should be prepared to challenge the wisdom of the West for we are no less wise.

Japan's present problem can be solved simply by fixing the exchange rate of the Yen. Indeed the world's economic problem can be largely resolved by removing the uncertainties which plague the exchange rates, particularly that which is brought about by currency trading. You are a heretic when you are alone. Christ was a heretic until his teachings were accepted. After that of course they burn at the stake anyone who did not accept the teachings of Christ. We will be heretics for a time but if exchange rates are made less volatile, world trade will increase and everyone will be more prosperous. Then the heretic will become a heretic no more.

The United States of America was founded by religious heretics and subsequently built up by political heretics. America will burn economic heretics today but we can be sure that eventually it will come to accept them.

America objects to the East Asia Economic Caucus. But Asians should persist. Asians should prove the EAEC is not only good for East Asia but also for the rest of the world. Asians should never think in terms of dominance, of dominating the world. And so the EAEC should preach the message of prospering the world. After all Asia cannot gain from impoverishing others. Only a prosperous world can buy what we produce. The EAEC should present itself as a partner for the other trade blocs; the European Union, NAFTA and the others. If we do and we prove that the EAEC is good for the whole world, we will not be burnt at the stakes. The world will embrace the EAEC and stop regarding it as a heresy.

If the EAEC is in place we would be able to resolve the East Timor problem eventually. Then East Timor would not be anyone's Vietnam.

CHAPTER 10

THE WORLD OF ISLAM

EVERYONE EXPECTED the Indonesian presidential election to be violent but in fact there was very little trouble. The election went off without serious incidents. And they also chose the President and Vice President very wisely, opting to work together rather than confronting each other. Every party of significance is in the Government. The choice of Gus Dur as President pacified the Muslim majority while Megawati's party which has the biggest number of seats but not an absolute majority seems satisfied to have the Vice Presidency. Even Golkar chose to join the coalition, accepting a number of ministerial posts. There seems to be reconciliation among the major parties and this augurs well for the future of Indonesia. Although Gus Dur's health is considered frail, he is supported by a strong team from his own party.

Indonesia's 220 million people is 90 per cent Muslim. It is in fact the biggest Muslim country in the world. However, Indonesians are quite diverse in their practice of Islam, some following rather relaxed interpretations, some more orthodox and some fairly rigid. They are not fanatical although the Achehnese tend to be very fierce in their defence of their religion, as the Dutch found out. So, there is a wide spectrum. It is different in Malaysia where the Malays are all Sunni Muslims who follow the teachings of Imam Shafei. Whatever may be the strength of the Indonesians' practice of Islam still they are Muslims and Indonesia is a Muslim country. So, it is natural that they would want to have a Muslim as their leader when they are given the choice. Had Megawati won with an absolute majority there would have been no choice. But although her party won the biggest number of seats, she would have to get the support of the other parties to have a majority and such support can only come from Muslim parties. This she could not get probably because Muslims generally do not like to be lead by women. Golkar's decision not to put up any candidate resulted in Gus Dur getting its support. Together with support from the other Muslim parties and the provincial representatives, Gus Dur was able to defeat Megawati. She could have opted to be in the opposition but wisely she chose to be Vice President. And so confrontation is avoided.

The ASEAN countries (Association of Southeast Asian Nations) all want Indonesia to have stability not only for Indonesia's sake but also for the good of the region. The relatively smooth elections and the wise choice of President and Vice President together with the decision of Golkar to participate in the Government should result in relative political stability in Indonesia.

There is a general feeling worldwide that Muslims tend to be extreme and violent. They cannot seem able to govern their countries well. They seem inclined towards terrorism. This is only partly true. Mostly it is due to media hype. When terrorism acts involve Muslims the terrorists are always described as "Muslim terrorists". Yet, there are Christian, Hindus and even Buddhist acts of terror but the terrorists are never linked to their religions. They are never referred to as Christian terrorists or Hindu terrorists or Buddhist terrorists.

Yet their terrorism is no less unthinking and violent than those of the Muslims. As a result of the media invariably referring to Muslim terrorists, most people have come to associate Islam and Muslims with terrorism. Even responsible Government leaders talk of Muslim terrorists and immediately point a finger towards them if any terrorist act occur as in the case of the bombing of a Government building in America which actually involved Christians.

In fact Muslims are the real victims of organised terror. In Bosnia Herzegovina, Kosovo, Chechnya, Palestine, Iraq, Iran and Libya, Muslims have been massacred, and bombed by anti Muslim groups and democratic Governments even. Hundreds of thousands of Muslims have been tortured, raped and killed. There is nothing they can do as not a single Muslim country is strong enough to protect Muslims, or even to protest over the ill-treatment and constant terrorising of the Muslims and their countries.

The oppression and terrorising of the Muslims and their countries have been going on for decades. The Muslims of Palestine have been expelled from their country for the past 50 years. Muslim grouse over Kashmir has never been given a real hearing. Even though the UN, for humanitarian reasons have allowed the exchange of Iraqi oil for medicine and food, very little of these much needed supplies have been allowed through. Instead Iraq has been indiscriminately and repeatedly bombed.

In the view of the Muslims, they are the victims of world-wide terrorism. They can seek no redress anywhere. They seem doomed to be the oppressed people forever.

Muslims are not the people who invented international terrorism. The first airplane hijacking was perpetrated by an American Christian. And many other innovative acts of terrorism were invented in the West. Even the Japanese were involved in the so-called Red Army in Germany. A well-known German terrorist group was the Baader-Meinhof gang.

They are no longer active but even today Muslim Turks are being killed by German racists.

Bitter and frustrated by their continued and worldwide oppression, unable to get any protection from anyone, the Muslims saw in the acts of terrorism invented by the Christian Europeans a means to hit back. If their countries cannot protect them, if the World Muslim Community cannot help them, then they must hit back the only way they can and that is by indiscriminate terror attacks. Terrorism offers them the only way to hit back at even the greatest military powers.

The cost to them is terrible. In Iraq their children are born deformed, their mortality rates very high because they are deprived of even simple medicine and are exposed to the strange effects of modern weapons. Grozny in Chechnya has been flattened by carpet bombing due to Russian retaliation. The Palestinians have been denied a homeland, have been jailed en masse and have been shot at and killed at random because their fight for their own country is described as terrorism.

The vast majority of the Muslims in the world are peaceful people. They are against terrorism. But they cannot help sympathising or at least understanding the bitterness of these people. In many instances they fear these so-called terrorists because they would be regarded as traitors if they go against them. Ordinary Muslims and even their Governments are not likely to actively suppress this violent fringe of their society. And so the acts of unthinking violence by these bitter and frustrated Muslims will continue.

Putting pressure on Muslim countries to curb the "terrorist" will not work. The people in Muslim countries will go against their Government and revolt if the Government acts against the terrorists. They would rather suffer than submit to foreign pressure.

So what can be done to curb "terrorist" acts by Muslims? In the first place stop talking of Muslim terrorists and Muslim terrorism. In many instances they are as much freedom fighters as the Africans who fought for independence through guerilla warfare who were also called terrorists until they gained independence. If there must be reference to Muslim terrorists there must also be reference to the religions of other terrorists.

Secondly the grievances of the Muslims and their countries, their sense of being oppressed, the attacks against their countries and people must be redressed. If action is to be taken against them it must be with UN sanction. Unilateral acts of terror against them by certain Governments only fuel their desire for revenge. It is important to remember that killing authorised by Governments are no less terrifying than killings by non-government groups. For the Muslim victims these are acts of terrorism.

And thirdly the media attacks and vilification of the Muslims and their countries should be balanced with factual reports against the non-Muslims who launch terror attacks on them. The Western media is responsible for stereotyping Muslims as fanatical mindless killers. The Muslims cannot be blamed if they think everyone is against them and as a result they harbour ill-feelings towards them.

Stop also the talk of the Islamic nuclear bomb. Many non-Muslim countries possess and test nuclear devices with impunity. Yet when Pakistan tested its nuclear device this is regarded as a threat to world peace. It should be remembered that Pakistan was not the first to test the device. Its neighbour and acknowledged enemy tested the device first. The Pakistanis have every right to fear India's bomb. Yet the world talks of the threat of Pakistan's bomb without considering the very real fears of the Pakistanis. For that matter the whole Muslim world feel threatened by the huge arsenal of nuclear weapons owned by the people who have no liking for them.

One should not of course forget that the US refuses to ratify the nuclear test-ban treaty. Yet the US has continued to punish the people of Iraq because there is a remote possibility that Iraq might have acquired the capability to produce the bomb. The fear of a Muslim nuclear capability is out of all proportion to their capacity to deploy this weapon. Muslims really have more reasons to fear the non-Muslims capacity to wipe them off the surface of this earth with the nuclear arsenal the non-Muslims possess. They have really no reason to believe there will be any more compassion when using this weapon against them than the compassion shown for Muslims in Bosnia, Kosovo or Chechnya.

I have learned from the media that during the dialogues with the gunmen holding Japanese hostages in Kyrgyzstan, Muslim countries played a big role in having the kidnapped people freed. This is indicative of the true concerns of Muslims about terrorist acts by their fellow Muslims. Responsible governments like that of Saudi Arabia try to clean up the image of Islam, as best they can. But it is a daunting task.

In Malaysia, we do have a Muslim party which tries to promote Islamic extremism. We curb them not by restricting their activities but by arguing with them in accordance with the teachings of Islam. The Quran and the traditions of the Prophet are against violence and instability in society. The Quran teaches the Muslims to be tolerant of the peoples of other religions. Muslims should only fight against non-Muslims if they are attacked first but if their attackers sue for peace then Muslims must choose the peaceful way. By and large the Muslims in Malaysia are willing to keep to the true teachings of Islam and reject the kind of fanaticism which leads to violance. That is why Malaysia is free from violence by Muslims and they are able to live in harmony with non-Muslims.

I believe that there is much that the Muslim countries and people can do to improve the image of Islam and the Muslims. The various groupings of the Muslim countries such as the

Organisation of Islamic Countries, the D-8 Group of Developing Islamic nations should help to refocus their people and Governments on the need to govern their countries well and to develop them so as to be able to compete with the other countries of the world.

We Muslims should prove that Islam is a religion for all times. We should reject the view that Islam is only for the 7th Century AD when Prophet Muhammad brought the message of Allah, the one and only God. Wearing clothings of the 7th century and rejecting modern knowledge, skills and technology will not make Muslims more Islamic. They must adhere closely to the faith and to the tenets of Islam but they must not reject the modern world.

Malaysian Muslims are able to adjust to the rapid progress of the modern world without losing or weakening their faith in Islam. Indeed their faith is very strong as can be seen by their steadfast performance of the rituals of faith and their adherence to the true teachings of Islam as found in the Holy Quran and the traditions of the Prophet. But their faith has in no way impeded them from building a modern industrialised country. Malaysian Muslims are able to Govern Malaysia together with non-Muslims and to be fair and just to everyone regardless of race or religion. Certainly Malaysian Muslims are not "terrorists".

The Muslims desire for peace is evident from their way of greeting. They say "Peace be upon you" when they meet each other or other people. Everywhere greetings between people express their innermost desires. Thus the Chinese who in the past experienced frequent famines greet each other by asking "Have you eaten". Japanese greet by asking "How is business". It is a measure of the Muslims desire for peace that they wish "peace" on whoever they meet. Unfortunately the modern world denies the peace the Muslims crave.

And so Muslims continue to feel bitter about their oppression by others and to try to hit back in their limited way.

CHAPTER 11

THE UGLY MALAYS

I AM VERY GLAD that we achieved the target of a two-thirds majority for the National Front in the Malaysian general election. But the Government's majority and the margins we won have been significantly reduced. We also failed to recapture one state and we lost another.

Four of my Cabinet members lost in the election. The opposition made inroads into Kedah, my home state. Selangor which had been an UMNO and Barisan Nasional stronghold lost a Parliamentary seat to PAS (Parti Islam SeMalaysia - Pan Malaysian Islamic Party) for the first time. Apparently quite a large proportion of Malays, the indigenous people of Malaysia, have turned against UMNO, their main political party.

Ordinarily a Government which had fended off a vicious attack on its economy and had turned around the economy so decisively would have gained the support of the people. In fact it does among the ethnic Chinese who are more involved in business. But the Malays did not really suffer from the currency and economic turmoil. There was no unemployment or shortages of supplies. In fact the devaluation of the currency meant they earned more 'Ringgit' from the palm oil they produce and export. For the Malays the issues are not economic. They are based on the perceptions of the new educated elite who had been exposed both to Western liberalism while studying abroad and to the more extreme variety of Islam as preached by PAS.

The focus on Western liberalism was initiated by my former deputy, Anwar Ibrahim. To get me to step down he had his supporters in the party to condemn alleged cronyism, nepotism and lack of transparency in the Government. He expected the attack to be supported so widely by the grassroot leaders of the party, especially at the 1998 UMNO General Assembly, that I would have to step down and he would take over as the annointed successor.

Unfortunately for him the Assembly gave full support to me. Nevertheless the outcry against the alleged misdeeds of the Government was picked up by opposition parties and by non-Governmental organisations.

Later when Anwar was removed from office following revelation that he was involved in unacceptable immoral activities, and he was subsequently arrested and charged for abuse of his authority, the opposition immediately whipped up popular support for him. His followers inside and outside the party and the opportunistic opposition took up his allegation that his removal was due to a conspiracy to prevent him from becoming the Prime Minister. His misbehaviour and breaches of the law were ignored even though he was tried in an open court. He succeeded in convincing his followers that the court was taking orders from the Prime Minister.

The educated elites, in particular the salaried professionals, assume that those in power and in a position to be corrupt must be corrupt. Proof of corruption is not necessary. Similarly the success of anyone in business, whether they are friends or children of the leaders or not must be due to cronyism and nepotism. They accordingly became anti-Government.

Many of the educated elites had been cultivated and even indoctrinated by PAS while they were still students. They became infused with anti-establishment sentiments. They immediately took up the defence of Anwar when he launched a campaign against alleged Government corruption etc., immediately after his removal from office. PAS and other opposition parties saw in the anti-Government campaign by Anwar an opportunity to gather more votes. Whether they believe in his innocence or not, the Anwar affair brought the opposition parties together in a loose coalition which effectively made the election a straight contest between two parties, the Barisan Nasional coalition versus the opposition coalition of four parties.

PAS benefited the most from this opposition coalition. The Democratic Action Party of extremely chauvinistic Chinese lost popularity because of its association with PAS and its proclaimed desire to set up an Islamic state. Keadilan, the party formed by Anwar, won only where PAS was strong and supported it for tactical reasons. The urban elites who wanted to achieve political position from exploiting the Anwar issue did not do well at all, although they did manage to reduce the majority of the Barisan Nasional candidates.

The Barisan Nasional won with a convincing two-thirds majority but lost two states to PAS. All the DAP leaders lost for the first time. Unless Anwar can somehow keep alive the issue of his jailing, Keadilan is not likely to survive the next five years.

In a way, the success of the Barisan Nasional's policies to reduce the economic disparity between the indigenous Malays and the Chinese contributed to its loss of Malay support. In 1969, race riots broke out in Kuala Lumpur after an election in which the Alliance, the predecessor of Barisan Nasional, did not do so well. The riots were sparked by a Chinese Party noisily celebrating its "victory" over the Malays. This provoked a similar celebration by the Malays. The two clashed violently with the Malays burning Chinese shop-houses and motor vehicles. For days Kuala Lumpur was unsafe for either Malays or Chinese.

The Government imposed a curfew and stopped the riots. But the bitterness of the Malays towards the Chinese and vice-versa appeared to be permanent. Everyone, Westerners in particular, predicted that Malaysia would never be peaceful again and that it would never develop.

The multi-racial leaders of the Alliance set out to repair the damage. Tracing the cause of racial animosity to the extreme disparity in the distribution of wealth between the races, an affirmative action policy, the New Economic Policy was formulated by which special effort would be made to help the Malays and other indigenous people catch up with the Chinese in the economic field. This was to be achieved by stimulating economic growth so that from the growth portion a greater amount could be allocated to the indigenous people. There would be no expropriation of the wealth of the Chinese.

To implement this policy the Government created hundreds of thousands of scholarships so that every Malay who has any ability at all would get education up to university level. Tens of thousands were sent abroad for further studies at tremendous cost. The universities at home accepted a higher proportion of Malays than non-Malays.

Through the issuance of business licences, easy loans, contracts, etc. budding Malay businessmen were given headstarts. Many failed of course but some made it and rose to become successful industrialists and top businessmen with interests worldwide.

By the 1990s the extreme disparity between the Chinese and the Malays was greatly reduced.

When the Barisan Nasional Government initiated the New Economic Policy, UMNO naively believed that the mainly Malay beneficiaries of this policy would be grateful or at least appreciative of what the party through the Barisan Nasional had done for them. They expect that from among the new elites there would be supporters and leaders who would carry on with the policy until its objectives are fully achieved.

Unfortunately, any gratefulness and appreciation were undermined by PAS which got at the students early and taught them that any Government would have done the same for them. They need not be grateful and thank the Barisan Nasional Government. They need not feel obliged to it in any way. They need only thank Allah (God), and nobody else, however instrumental they may be in creating and distributing the benefits.

That this is against the true teachings of Islam does not bother PAS. Once the sense of obligation towards a paternalistic UMNO-led Government is destroyed, PAS is able to gain unquestioned support by claiming that PAS is Islam and all Muslims must support PAS. From then on PAS could tell lies and even denigrate God and it would still retain the unstinted support of its members and followers. It is no exaggeration to say that for its followers and supporters believing in PAS is a matter of faith, not political belief.

The collaboration between PAS and the Chinese chauvinists of the DAP was also accepted without question by PAS followers. The Chinese on the other hand rejected DAP because its alliance with PAS is seen by them as support for Muslim extremists who advocate an Islamic state in which the Chinese would be second class citizens subjected to Islamic laws.

There are other reasons for UMNO losing quite a considerable amount of support from the Malays. Definitely there is the arrogance of power, not always confined to leaders in the Government but also among other party leaders and even ordinary members. Intra-party squabbles caused by personal rivalries and disappointment over being passed over as candidates also weakened the party. There may be other reasons which need to be identified.

Basically after four decades of prosperity the Malays have come to believe that nothing can now diminish their dominant position in Malaysian politics. They believe that they need not be united any more nor do they need Government patronage. Such is their confidence that even when PAS denounced the affirmative action in favour of the Malays, they remain loyal to PAS.

Under the British, very few Malays could get a university education. I was one of the fortunate few. The non-Malay students outnumbered the Malays ten to one. Today, any Malay at all can get a scholarship to the university. If they are not qualified, the government provides special coaching so that they can get into university with minimal qualifications. So, it is not a privilege any more to get a scholarship and to go to the university. It has become a right for them. If you feel that it is a right, then you don't feel grateful to the Government. Since there is no sense of obligation, they don't even feel a need to study hard. They get deeply involved in partisan politics. They usually perform badly in their studies. It is not that Malays are not intelligent but without studying no one can perform well.

The Government will have to assess the situation, to see whether Malays are really competent to compete on their own. If they are, of course the Government has to cease helping them. On the other hand, if the Malays are not, they need to continue to have Government support. It is possible that the Malays have become complacent because they are doing well. It is possible that they only imagine that they are capable. Personally, I don't think they are. They still need to be given handicaps, given headstarts. Once the affirmative action is abandoned, it cannot be brought back again.

Actually, I was planning to call the elections for January 2000, after the Muslim fasting month. But then PAS is likely to use the various religious functions during that month to poison the minds of the Muslims against the Government. People will not be able to perform their religious duties in peace. I had to rethink. I had gone around the country, and noted that our supporters' spirits were high and they were ready. I doubted I could improve it anymore. It didn't take long to decide. I didn't consult with anybody. Not even my wife knew. She was preparing herself to go to South Africa for the Commonwealth Heads of Government Meeting which I was attending.

The Western press as expected condemned the Malaysian government for being unfair to the opposition parties, of not having freedom of the press, etc during the elections. Even the capture of two states by PAS and an increase in their number of elected representatives have not convinced the West that the election is fair. The fact is that the Western press can see nothing right about the Malaysian Government. My propensity to criticise them and Western countries has not endeared me to them. They like to have Asian leaders submit to Western bullying. It is not whether we are democratic or just or fair that they are concerned about. They have been known to support dictators if they are aligned to the West. Their negative reaction is therefore only to be expected. I have long ago ceased to care about what the Western media says about our country.

The fact that Malaysia has succeeded in maintaining peace and harmony in this multi-racial country, the fact that we have managed to overcome the attacks by the currency traders on our own has merely made the Western media more angry. We will therefore continue to draw adverse comments from them.

Democracy is the best political system invented by Man. However it is far from perfect. Parties vying for elected seats often abuse the system. Religious faith can be misdirected in order to gain support. Bribes are offered and in Malaysia Muslims are promised heaven in the afterlife if they vote for the Islamic Party. Unpopular but necessary legislations have to be aborted for fear of losing support. Sometimes in a two-party system a small majority can lead to an ineffective Government due to fear of defections. Strikes and riots can stifle progress. Instead of benefiting the people democracy can stunt growth, impoverish and even lead to domination by neo-imperialists.

I am grateful that so far Malaysia has been able to practise democracy and remain peaceful and stable and to develop reasonably fast. I am not sure that this will always be so. The recent election shows that lies and bribes and empty promises for the afterlife can win seats and put unprincipled people in power.

CHAPTER 12

THE CAPITALISM WORLD

MALAYSIA ENTERED year 2000, the first year of the 21st century and third millennium determined to achieve its objective of becoming a fully developed country by the year 2020. Some have wondered why 2020 and not some other year. As a doctor I am attracted to the optometrist measurement of vision; 2020 indicate 100 percent good vision in both eyes. Our Vision 2020 for Malaysia implies this clear vision of where we want to go and what we want to be.

Our confidence and determination to achieve this vision is based on our record of development since independence. In the 10 years before the economic turmoil of 1997-1998 we were growing at eight percent plus, higher than our seven percent growth target needed to double our per capita every 10 years for 30 years. Even if growth for the next 10 years averages slightly less than seven percent we would still be on target. We think we can grow at that rate barring a major catastrophe.

In addition we had successfully overcome the financial and economic turmoil following the attack by currency traders and short-term stock market speculators. We were very strong financially when we were attacked in 1997. Our savings rate has always been high at almost 40 percent of GDP while our foreign debts, both public and private were very low.

When we imposed foreign exchange control we succeeded because we had little need to borrow from foreign sources. We borrowed from Japan of course but that was necessary to restart some infrastructure projects where we need to import various components. Today the economy is fully turned around, with reserves 50 percent higher than prior to the turmoil and the stock market fully recovered. We grew by more than four percent in 1999 and expect more than five percent in 2000.

In the recent elections we retained our two-thirds majority, actually winning three-fourth of the seats. But analysis of the results has shown worrying trends.

The 14 party National Front Coalition has my party, the United Malays National Organisation (UMNO), as its core. This party has always had strong support from the indigenous Malays. Whereas the Chinese and Indian supported the Barisan Nasional strongly in this election, Malay support has been very significantly eroded.

Our studies show that the indigenous Malays have now become complacent. They were very far behind the other races in the early days of independence, owning only two percent of the economic wealth of the country, and had very few educated at university level. Their participation in business was minimal and they held only junior posts in the Government.

As a result of the New Economic Policy of affirmative action in favour of the indigenous people they now have 20 percent of economic wealth and hundreds of thousands of them have university qualifications and besides being in various professions they own numerous successful businesses ranging from small to medium to very big corporations. They have now become so confident of their own ability that they see no need to be grateful to the Government which had given them a headstart. Instead they have become very critical of the Government and agreed with allegations by Western people that it is corrupt, practices cronyism and is not transparent.

Part of this disillusionment with the present Government and the UMNO in particular is due to the previous Deputy Prime Minister building a personal following in preparation for his attempt to overthrow myself as the President of UMNO and Prime Minister. His fanatical followers are very angry over his removal from Government for moral depredation and his subsequent conviction by the courts for corrupting police officers. They believe his story that his removal and subsequent trials on various charges were due to a huge conspiracy by Party and Government leaders to prevent him from becoming Prime Minister of Malaysia. They therefore turned against the UMNO during election. Pictures of the black eye that the ex-Deputy Prime Minister got because of the alleged beating by the Inspector-General of Police were displayed all over the country and caused great anger against the Government.

The Anwar factor together with a vicious campaign by the Pan Malaysian Islamic Party (PAS) that UMNO Malays are not Muslims resulted in defeat of a number of UMNO candidates in marginal seats.

Besides this rather poor performance by UMNO, the success of the New Economic Policy in bringing up the Malays to a higher level of development has also brought about a change in the character of the Malays. They think that they no longer need to work hard as they will always be dominant and will always succeed in Malaysia. They are somewhat like the younger generation of Japanese who are not so dedicated to work and the success of the country. This new attitude will result in the failure of our affirmative action to help the Malays catch up with the other races and they may once again become the deprived in their own country.

The split in the Malay ranks, their new confidence and their lack of dedication to education and work can slow down our progress and make our Vision 2020 unachieveable. We now have to devote more time to reawakening the spirit of the early years of independence and to explain away the misconceptions and misunderstandings of the Malays about Government policies. For example we have to explain why we are carrying out big projects. Western critics have accused us of wasting money on the so-called mega projects and the Malays have joined the foreigners in this criticism.

Actually although the projects are big they are not mega in terms of irresponsible waste of funds. Size is relative. A small project for a poor country can be considered a waste. But so-called mega projects in Malaysia are well within our means. If they are wasteful we would be in grave financial trouble today. But we are so strong financially that we did not have to run to the IMF to borrow money during the financial crisis recently. We pulled this country out of the economic recession and financial turmoil using our own financial strength, in spite of predictions by world experts that our economy would collapse. The Chinese and Indian Malaysian understand and appreciate this. But we have to explain to the Malays who seem to have more faith in foreigners than in their own people as leaders of Government.

Malaysian 2020 Vision has influenced many countries to have long term visions of their own. ASEAN too have a 2020 Vision i.e. to become a much more integrated grouping and to develop into an ASEAN free trade area or AFTA. Unfortunately membership of APEC has undermined ASEAN solidarity. Each ASEAN country seems to have an independent stand as a member of the APEC. In fact commitment to APEC seems to supercede commitment to ASEAN. Perhaps APEC is more glamorous as the world's most powerful and richest country is a member and is represented by its top leaders.

APEC's principal interest is in opening up the markets of member countries, and we know the market potential of China, Korea and the Southeast Asian countries is huge. But Southeast Asian countries and Korea have since learnt that opening markets pose serious threats. The attacks on the currencies and stock markets by mainly American speculators have raised doubts about the benefits of market opening, globalisation and the borderless world. We also find that the IMF is not capable of handling the effects of such attacks. Not only did the countries which were attacked suffer economic recession following the attacks and devaluation of their currencies, but the whole world suffered from a recession. Clearly the IMF cannot be regarded as an effective guardian of the world's finances. Nor can the present financial regime guarantee that no more attacks will be made by currency traders against the economies of countries in order to rake in huge profits for themselves.

Today we are still seeing damaging fluctuations in the exchange rates of many countries brought about by the currency traders. The Japanese Yen has appreciated by 20 percent resulting in difficulties for countries buying Japanese goods or paying off Yen loans.

Currency trading is said to be 20 times bigger than world trade. Whereas world trade creates businesses, jobs, insurance, freight transportation and a host of other activities, there is nothing to show that currency trading has done anything for anyone else other than the traders and the share holders of the hedge funds. If world trade is 20 times bigger than what it is now we can be sure that the world would be 20 times more prosperous. But currency trading, far from increasing prosperity, has severely impoverished countries and regions, causing millions to lose their jobs, riots and strikes, political and social instability.

The time has come for the world to rethink about the

International Financial regime. Must we allow currency traders to determine the exchange rates of our money or should we find a new mechanism to determine exchange rates? Interventions by Central Bank has been shown to be costly and ineffective. Maybe we should go back to the fixed exchange rate. In the early years of the Bretton Woods the exchange rates were fixed and recovery from the war was rapid. Why is it that we are not allowed to even think about fixed exchange rates at all now? Why must we protect the rights of currency traders to abuse the exchange rate mechanism.

When Malaysia decided to look East, we did so because we admired the way Japan was able to recover from the ravages of war. But today Japan seem unable to overcome its economic problems. We think that the difficulty is due to your too strong commitment to the Western system including the floating exchange rates which is strongly supported by the U.S. and is its main beneficiary. Your own system of business including your life-time employment, your strong linkages and the strong cooperation between Government and business are good and had contributed to your rapid recovery and growth. Now you have suddenly discarded all your systems in order to adopt Western systems. The result is a prolonged recession from which you are only just recovering.

I have travelled to Japan very many times and have seen the tremendous progress you have made. But during my last visit I was appalled to see your unemployed people living in makeshift shelters of blue plastic sheets in the cities of Japan. This is no doubt the result of doing away with life-time employment. Now your Corporations are being bought by foreigners and their first action to improve efficiency is to dismiss workers and close down factories. If this is the solution to revive the business surely you can do the sacking yourself.

Perhaps Western business practices are better than Japanese practices, although Japan has become the second biggest economy in the world through your own system of finance and business. Perhaps you can do better with Western systems. But there is no doubt that by adopting Western practices your economy is not doing so well and so many of your people are unemployed. If you must adopt Western practices shouldn't it be done slowly so as to minimise damage to your economy. It seems to me that you feel guilty about your system that you have to throw it out overnight. Sudden change like this must be destructive even if the change is for the better.

What I see happening today as a result of globalisation is an attempt to set up worldwide monopolies of certain businesses by a few giant corporations mainly from the West. In the future there will be at the most five banks, five automotive companies, five hypermarkets, five hotel chains, five restaurant chains and so on, all operating worldwide. All the small and medium-sized companies in these fields and maybe others too will be absorbed by these Western-owned international giants. These monopolies would, it is claimed, bring about efficiency and thus lowering cost through economies of scale. The raw materials the world needs will also be produced by giant mining and plantation companies operating in poor countries, and will be carried by air and sea freighters belonging to giant transportation companies, to be processed and resold throughout the world. Some of course will use cheap labour in the poor countries in order to reduce cost.

It is the dream world of the super capitalists come true. Others will merely work for the capitalists. They will earn more but they will own nothing that they can call their own. Quite obviously the great capitalists will wield immeasurable power. And they will become corrupted as they manipulate Governments and international agencies so as to enable them to make more and more money for themselves.

When the Cold War ended with the defeat of Communism, it was not democracy which won. It was Capitalism with a big capital C. The advent of Communism and Socialism in the early years of the 20th Century forced

Capitalism to adopt a more human face. Monopolies were broken up and curbed. Today, without the challenge of Communism, the true ugliness of Capitalism has revealed itself. This time it will not permit any opposition or restriction.

Democracy, the rule of the majority and the concern for the poor and the small must not stand in the way of world-girdling unbridled Capitalism. Through the IMF, the WTO, the international media and the power of the most powerful and richest country on earth, Capitalism will assert its power.

Before this juggernaut all must fall. The question is do we resist now before it is too late or do we wait until, like Communism, millions have been sacrificed before we rise in rebellion.

Malaysia is a small weak country with its many problems. Maybe we are too pessimistic, too fanciful. But our recent bout with the currency traders has made us suspicious and wary of new ideas and the promises made by others.

CHAPTER 13

THE ASIAN VALUES

I HAD BILATERAL meeting with French President, Jacques Chirac in Paris recently. We talked about economic ties between our countries as well as our links to Japan. We also discussed how Malaysia, France and Japan can help the development of human resources in African countries. Chirac was very interested in how we overcame the economic crisis. He understood — and backed — Malaysia's need to introduce currency controls. I have known him a long time since the days he was mayor of Paris. He is open minded. He listens to people. He wants to know about people. He doesn't just lecture. He asks good questions — he asked how Malaysia avoided seeking International Monetary Fund assistance during the crisis.

I had lunch with him for about two hours. For Malaysians, we respect French culture and have no objection to them drinking wine or liquor during meals with us. We are fine with water or apple juice. Even if the French serve wine, we just don't drink it. When we have guests coming from overseas, we propose a toast with apple juice. We don't serve alcoholic drinks in Malaysia or at receptions abroad. The only thing that we request when we are invited for dinner in other countries is that they should not serve pork — even for themselves. We are brought up to think that pork is unclean and it upsets us to have pork served at our table. Most people, who are not Muslims know this and did not mind respecting our feelings.

We believe that we have to respect other peoples' culture so that they will respect ours. They respect you by not serving pork, but we respect that in their culture they have wine with their meals. We don't go around saying, 'your way is wrong, our way is right'. But there is a limit. For example in Western culture, they accept homosexuality, including promoting homosexual practices among school children. We cannot accept this. We admit that some people are born with their sexuality mixed up. That is not their fault. But to promote homosexual practices actively as is being done in some European countries is to purposely promote abnormality. We will not accept this in our country as our religion is strongly against it. In Europe homosexual ministers must be invited together with their same sex partners. That is their business. We will not invite them that way. They can come alone.

In a country in which 100 per cent of the population is Muslim, the application of Muslim laws is usually very rigid — even with foreigners. In a country where Muslims are a minority such as in Latin America, the Muslims cannot insist that non-Muslims cover their faces as would be done in a country in which 100 per cent of the population is Muslim. Clearly the practices of Muslim injunctions differ according to the circumstances. In Malaysia, we have lived with people of different races and religions for centuries. We learn by example, from our parents and other on how to conduct our relations. We don't have any problems if our neighbours are Chinese or Indians and have different religious practices. We don't quarrel because our religious practices are different. On Malaysia's west coast, people are more used to mixing with different ethnic groups. On the east coast, the majority is Muslim and Malay — so they tend to be more rigid. Their ability to tolerate other people is less. When Muslims are seemingly flexible they are not deviating from the teaching, of Islam. Islam permits differences in practice according to the circumstance.

Although I am a Malay and a Muslim, that does not prevent me from admiring and wanting to copy the ways of others as long as they are not proscribed by religion. And so I admire Chinese culture and the teachings of Confucius with the stress on filial piety, commitment to hard work, strong sense of community etc. The Chinese give less priority to immediate needs. They think over the long term. And so they are willing to make sacrifices in order to gain later. That is why the Chinese have thrived and prospered wherever they are.

I also admire Western culture, which believes in organisation. For example, the Portuguese were able to conquer Malacca even though their forces were small. They were better organised and the line of command was clear. They were more disciplined and methodical. On the other hand the army of the Malay Sultan was not properly organised, had no training and it was not clear as to who was in command. Although a bigger force equipped with elephants they were defeated by the Portuguese.

Besides being organised the Europeans are more methodical. In research they would examine every part and every possibility one by one instead of doing things at random. Europeans are also curious and want to explore and find out things. And when they find something new they will want to study its application. Hence the advancements made in science by the Europeans.

When Japan occupied Malaysia during World War II, the soldiers were very disciplined, brave and patriotic, which I admire. I used to sell goods in the market; Japanese soldiers always paid for all they bought. The cultivation of good values that will contribute towards achieving one's goals is something that must be learnt by everyone. The younger generation must appreciate this if they wish to succeed. You cannot succeed by always wanting to do what you like or feel inclined to do.

In Indonesia, there are many different races and religions. After the crisis in that country, the situation has become very difficult. It is a country in transition. It has accepted democracy. Democracy is not so easily understood, nor practised. People may not know the limits of democracy. Because of that, even if the government wants to introduce good things, it may not be able to do so. It will take time for Indonesia to resolve this difficult situation.

I have known Indonesia's General Wiranto for some time. He is a well trained, disciplined soldier. He shows quite dignity as a military officer. I think the military anywhere should be professional and non-partisan and Indonesia's military can provide stability for Indonesia. Without stability, it will be difficult for Indonesia to progress towards democracy. I think that the military will continue to play a diminishing role over the years, until Indonesian people master democracy. When everybody realises that this transition is difficult and are willing to make compromises, things will be all right.

The problem of Indonesia is that people lost a tremendous amount of wealth during the crisis. My belief is that you cannot be too rigid in trying to correct past practices that were bad. Everything takes time. You cannot take money from somebody and say, 'Now behave yourself'. The only thing that person will do is to fight back. If a person has no money, there is nothing for that person to lose. He will be very irresponsible and aggressive.

The IMF can be more relaxed on things. They keep on saying that if you don't do this, we will not give you money. That is forcing the Indonesians to do things that may not be good for the nation. I think ethnic Indonesian Chinese should go back to Indonesia. They must learn to truly share the wealth of Indonesia with all the indigenous people. At the same time, ethnic Chinese in Indonesia should have certain assurances that they will be protected from any violence. As a member of the Association of Southeast Asian Nations, Malaysia worries very much about what is going on in Indonesia. We wish to see Indonesia once again stable and prosperous. It will be good for its Asean neighbours.

I also had a meeting with East Timor's Jose Alexander Gusmao, a man tipped to become the President of that nation together with Ramos Horta, his colleague. He is a friendly person. He talked about the kind of a country the Timorese wish to rebuild. They need help to develop an administrative and a diplomatic corps. We have been helping out new countries like Commonwealth of Independent States in these fields. We are willing to do the same for East Timor. As long as East Timor is stable, then it can reconstruct itself. I think they will be able to overcome their problems. They are interested in forgetting the past and to look to the future. Gusmao knows about Malaysia's development. He seems to think that Malaysia is a good model country. We are willing to help them.

CHAPTER 14

GLOBALISATION

DURING the United Nations Conference on Trade and Development (UNCTAD) in Bangkok, Malaysia related once again its experience in dealing with currency trading and its views on new ideas such as globalisation, a borderless world, liberalisation and the free market. All these things which are said to be good for the world, can bring a lot of harm unless redefined and the stages of development of different countries are taken into consideration. As it is these concepts are invented and interpreted by the developed countries for their own good. We are therefore asking that the developing countries be allowed to reinterpret them so as to ensure that the benefits are evenly shared between the rich and the poor.

Indonesian President Abdurrahman Wahid made a speech off the cuff, after I made my speech. He made many references to the matters I brought up. He openly said that Indonesia is weak and is under the direction of the International Monetary Fund (IMF). He is not in a position to do anything but to take orders from it. Even though his country has no say against such a powerful organisation, he said that his country and his people will maintain their dignity. That is why he said that the role of UNCTAD is very important. It brings together the big powers and the small countries. Indonesia had a similar experience to those of other Asian countries during the financial crisis, perhaps they suffered even more from the new ideas, like the free flow of capital across borders, which are part of globalisation.

At the UNCTAD meeting, we managed to expose further the harm that these new concepts and ideas can do to the small economies. This time the response was quite good. Many leaders and officials were not only interested but also gave open support and repeated the points that we made. To that extent, UNCTAD was a success.

It is clear that the developed countries were shocked and bitter over the violent protest against globalisation and free trade at the meeting of the World Trade Organisation (WTO) in Seattle, Washington. If this had happened in a developing country, they would have said that it was due to the usual ignorance and emotional reaction of the people in such countries. But this happened in one of their own countries and involved many of their own people. They cannot ignore such opposition. In addition to this, many influential people well-versed in economics and other disciplines have come around to accept that free-trade and globalisation may not be the best thing for the world and that there can be other ways of tackling economic problems and these can also work.

When we implemented our idea of currency controls, we were condemned by all. We were told that it would not work and that it would bring about economic disaster for us. But we have proven that it can work and now many are using it as an example of how to resolve financial and economic problems. There are some who say that we would have recovered anyway as we implemented our controls just when the recession had bottomed out. If we look at the back numbers of the great economic magazines of the West we would see that they were predicting further regression of the economies of East

Asia at the time we imposed our controls. If there was recovery at that time it was because the currency traders and others feared that any further devaluation may push other Asian countries into doing what Malaysia did. In fact the fear was actually expressed that other countries would follow in Malaysia's footsteps. This would be disastrous for the currency trading business. They quickly stopped devaluing the currencies of East Asian countries, thus allowing these countries to recover together with Malaysia. Besides the IMF decided to relax its conditions and allowed its client states to reduce interest rates and ignore its instructions to have a budget surplus.

Cronyism and corruption did not result in currencies being devalued. These practices had been there all the time and did not prevent the East Asian countries from growing economically. The devaluation of the currencies was entirely due to manipulation by the currency traders.

Cronyism and corruption are found everywhere and are more rampant in the developed countries. The bailing out of the American Long Term Credit Management Fund is a good example. But beyond that the powerful countries use their influence on crony countries and client states, in order to get contracts for their companies and also to get them to support their policies internationally. This is cronyism and corruption at the highest level.

The West likes to use the phrase level playing field. They ignore the fact that even on a level field, if the teams are not evenly matched, it is far from fair. If you make adults play American football against little children from developing countries, the children will never win. The level playing fields are invented by the rich countries to legitimise unfair competition. The international press which they control then try to justify the fairness of a level playing field. Even the developing countries have to use the Western media as their own news agencies cannot cover world events. As a result the slanted views of the West are aired everywhere. What truly happened during the currency crisis in East Asia has never been correctly reported. Control of the world media by a few ultra rich individuals from the West is unhealthy and undemocratic.

I met the WTO Secretary-General Mike Moore. I heard from other countries that there would be no ministerial meeting of the WTO this year, so there will be no progress in trade negotiations. He says that he is making an effort to get people to better understand the WTO and its objectives. But people are not ready to accept the ideas which are being pushed by the WTO. The practice of holding a meeting that is not open but is confined to a few countries is objectionable. At these meetings small countries are not heard, except perhaps those under the influence of Western capitalist countries. We believe that globalisation should be reinterpreted. Why is globalisation confined only to the flows of money, and the rights of companies to operate worldwide without restriction? Why are these companies merging and acquiring other corporations and becoming so huge that it looks like the world will have only a small number of companies and there will be oligopolies in all industries and businesses? We fear this because they are so big and powerful that they will operate like the seven sisters in the oil industry did prior to the creation of OPEC (the Organisation of Petroleum Exporting Countries) when they controlled the world market and determined the prices. They kept the oil producing countries poor by paying them only 20 cent for a barrel. The rich world burnt the fuel furiously as it was so cheap.

We feel that globalisation is being used as an excuse to do away with national economic activities. They will one day force the national stock exchanges to close down and replace them with one stock exchange based in Wall Street. Internet stock trading has shown that this is possible. Every business activity will be controlled by very powerful companies controlled by the rich. They do not mind losing money in a small country because they can make money in other places. If national companies or banks lose money that will be the end of them. The big international companies can then buy national companies cheaply.

We are now supporting former Japanese Ministry of Finance Vice Minister for International Affairs Dr Eisuke Sakakibara in his bid to run for the IMF managing director's post. The IMF, in our view, hasn't done a good job. It is too rigid and Eurocentric. It is not looking at the world as a whole but from the view of Europe or America. It cannot understand Asian ways. For the IMF there is only one way. We need to have a person with a broader world view, not confined to just one ethnic group. We need a person who can accept that different people have different ways of doing things. Sakakibara has enough experience. He has a Western education and is very familiar with Europeans and Americans, as well as Asians. He is holistic in his view point, and does not confine himself to a narrow need.

I know it will be very difficult for him to get the position, because the way international civil servants are chosen is not democratic. We don't have a say in the IMF or the World Bank, simply because we are weak. There is a lot of talk about democracy. However, when it comes to international organisations like the United Nations one vote from one country doesn't count. In reality, only five countries decide what to do. This is supposed to be a democratic organisation, but it is really an oligopoly. Only a few people run the whole show. However these same people condemn others for not being democratic.

During UNCTAD, I had a chance to meet ASEAN (Association of Southeast Asian Nations) heads of state. I was surprised when Singapore Prime Minister Goh Chok Tong strongly proposed that East Asian countries should have a formal organisation, not just a periodic conference. We should have a formal organisation like NAFTA or EU even and hold regular meetings. We need to look into our common problems especially in our relations with groupings like NAFTA (the North American Free Trade Agreement) and the European Union.

When Malaysia proposed the East Asia Economic Group (EAEG), Japan was very reluctant to support it. I believe this is because Japan does not want to be accused of trying to revive its Greater East Asia Co-prosperity Sphere, proposed during the Pacific War. The Japanese people are very sensitive about this War and seems to feel perpetually guilty. They are always apologising for the War. The EAEG reminds them of this East Asia Co-prosperity Sphere and Japanese imperialism. China and Korea also remember this and yet China is supportive of the EAEG. I should remind Japan and everyone that the EAEG is not a Japanese creature. It is an idea proposed by Malaysia. There is no need for Japan to feel guilty about reviving a wartime objective. Similarly Japan should not be reluctant to play a leading role in Asia. We have only Japan as a member of the G-7. If Japan does not champion us then who will?

In Europe, Germany took the initiative in forming the European Union. Germany is the strongest partner in the European Union. Even in finance, the Bundesbank determined the exchange rate, the progress toward the Euro currency. Yet Germany hasn't apologised about the last war, not even to Israel. So, Japan can do the same. Japan was mislead by the Japanese militarists, which had an ambitious plan to dominate us. Just as the Germans blame the Nazis why cannot Japan blame the militarists? However, Japan must not deny what it did during the war. Japan has to teach the real history to its young generation. But the world cannot penalise forever this generation of Japanese because of what was done by their parents or grandparents 50 years ago. If we looked at our history that way, our relationship with our neighbours will always be bad. Malaysia cannot have any dealings with

Thailand or Indonesia, because we once fought against them. But we are friends now.

During the meeting between the Japanese Prime Minister Keizo Obuchi and other ASEAN leaders, we gave our views to him so that he could bring them to the attention of G-8 leaders at the Summit meeting to be held in Okinawa. We pointed out that the G-8 had in the past made decisions which affected the economies of smaller countries adversely, as for example the revaluation of the Yen. The debts of many countries doubled as a result.

Some of us also stressed the strong need for a regional fund. I supported this idea of an Asian Regional Fund. We do not believe that such a regional fund would affect the IMF or the World Bank. After all the Asian Development Bank and other regional development banks had not affected the World Bank. The idea that there should be only one fund for the whole world is without any sound basis. If there is enough money available we can have several funds. Such funds should be used to help countries in financial trouble. It should not be for promoting any country's political agenda.

When a country has real financial problems, it may be due to bad management, or too much foreign borrowing, or poor performance by the world's economy which affects exports, etc. At that stage, the fund can come in, and the fund managers can advise on how to resolve the problem. The advice should not be standard like that offered by the IMF. I think we have the capacity to do that. We have enough experience. We can prevent countries from going under. Because we believe that failure of any country in the region can affect the whole region, we must come to the rescue immediately. We must recognise the signs of impending recession and try to prevent it. There are sufficient indicators to help us foresee economic downturns. We should have our own people, interacting together. Then it will work.

The fund itself should be subscribed to by all countries,

according to their ability. I wouldn't like this fund to be too closely associated with Japan. Therefore, it should be located in another country. That way, people will not say it is Japanese fund but a regional fund. If the fund is located in a developing country it will help the economic development of that country. The fund will draw a lot of activities, including a lot of visitors to the country.

Some people now say that as it has been one and half years since we introduced the currency controls and they have worked, we should lift the controls. But the international community has not formulated a new financial architecture to curb currency manipulation by the currency traders. If we lift control our currency will again be at risk of wildly fluctuating exchange rates.

We are not going to change the Ringgit's exchange rate according to our whims and fancies. This is not good for business. A steady exchange rate lowers cost by making hedging unnecessary. It also helps business budgeting. Only when it is absolutely necessary will we change the exchange rate of the Malaysian Ringgit.

CHAPTER 15

ONE-CHINA POLICY

THE TAIWANESE people elected Mr Chen Shui-bian as the new President of Taiwan. He advocates independence for Taiwan. It is obvious that the majority of Taiwanese people want to be on their own. But it is quite unlikely that China would allow them to be independent. They will eventually have to be content with more autonomy such as that enjoyed by the people of Hong Kong.

In Indonesia there are many provinces which would like to become independent states. But nations cannot allow secession of the provinces because there will be more demands and in the end the nations will break up and will be succeeded by numerous small and non-viable states, which can be exploited by foreign powers.

We experienced something similar in Malaysia. When we were trying to form Malaysia in 1963, we had hoped Brunei would join. Brunei is very rich because of the oil that it produces. Brunei naturally expected to retain its oil wealth if it joined Malaysia. But this would be contrary to the Malaysian Government policy. In the end Brunei did not join Malaysia as the terms were not suitable for it. This is of course not quite like demanding for independence but clearly local sensitivities can become an impediment to unity.

Relations between Brunei and Malaysia became strained after this. Brunei suspected that Malaysia was fomenting unrest because several Brunei dissidents had been given asylum in Malaysia. It took a long time for the rift to be healed.

Singapore was very bullish about joining Malaysia as the PAP Government hoped to be accepted as a part of the Central Government. But the Alliance Government refused to share power with the PAP which was not a member of the Alliance. The PAP then launched a campaign for equal rights for all Malaysians irrespective of racial origins. This would result in the indigenous Malays and others becoming the deprived in their own country. Using the slogan Malaysian Malaysia the PAP tried to agitate the Chinese population to reject the socio political contract between the races entered into during the struggle for independence in which the special position of the indigenous people was recognised by the Chinese and Indians. As a result of the PAP campaign the relation between the Malays and the Chinese became very tense. There were demonstrations by the Malays in Singapore. In the end the Prime Minister, Tunku Abdul Rahman, decided that Singapore with its largely Chinese population was not compatible with Malaysia's spirit of sharing between the different races and Singapore was expelled.

The expulsion of Singapore from Malaysia is not quite the same as secession but it does show that people usually think largely of their own interest and not of the whole nation. The fact that they may be of the same race or origin does not necessarily make them want to stay united, to help each other and to strengthen the nation. They would rather have a small nation where their own interest is upheld than be a part of a strong big nation.

I suppose it is the same in Taiwan. On the one hand, the Taiwanese people feel that they are Chinese. On the other hand, they don't want to lose control of the better life that they now have in Taiwan. Maybe China's one nation two systems can provide a solution. It seems to have worked in Hong Kong. Whatever the solution it is up to the Chinese people to decide.

As far as Malaysia is concerned, the fact that there is a new government in Taiwan, which is much more pro-independence than was the previous government, does not mean that we will abandon our support for the One-China policy. We have always regarded Taiwan as a part of China. It is a fact of history. It so happens that the Nationalists retreated to Taiwan, and that cannot change the fact of geo-political history. The Nationalists also retreated to northern Thailand and Burma but China has not claimed sovereignty over these territories.

Chinese Premier Zhu Rongji delivered a strong message before the election that China will use any means to stop the separatists. It was difficult for Zhu to say otherwise as that may be taken to indicate that it was prepared to abandon its One-China policy. He cannot be seen to be tolerating the setting up of two Chinas. From the regional point of view if there are two Chinas, there will always be tension. Whatever the policies of the new administration in Taiwan, Malaysia will not recognise it as an independent country. We will regard it as a trading entity and our relations will be based on that.

I met Lee Teng-hui once in the late 1980s when I went to Taiwan. Like all politicians I believe he had to pander to domestic politics even though he knew that Taiwan's independence is not compatible with the realities outside of the country. In the end his candidate was rejected by the Taiwanese even though his stand had annoyed the mainland Chinese. But it must be admitted that the Kuomintang (Nationalist) Party did a good job developing Taiwan economically. Lee can take some of the credit for this.

From the beginning Taiwan adopted the free market capitalistic system. There was no central planning as in the mainland where for a long time the Communist ideology and system prevailed. As a result Taiwan prospered and became one of the Asian Tigers. Some of the biggest shipping corporations in the world are owned by Taiwanese, as are some of the most successful industries such as computer manufacturer Acer. China can benefit a lot from the entrepreneurship and business skills of the Taiwanese. They can help China adjust to the free market system and integrate itself fully with the world's economy.

Mr. Chen, may have been elected for his pro-independence stand but now that he has won he will find a need to face reality. All politicians have to modify their stand once they win and shoulder responsibility for the well-being of their country. Promises can easily be made when you are in the opposition and have no responsibility to carry out the promises. But the rhetorics will have to be abandoned when faced with the realities of running a Government and the country. I believe that Mr Chen and his party will modify their stand and seek to review their stand on independence.

The problem that will plague the Government of Taiwan will be foreign interference. Outside powers will want to use it to achieve their own national agenda. It will be in the interest of these powers to see that China and Taiwan remains hostile towards each other. Wishing to retain friends is natural for a country that is isolated but it would be unwise to confront China in furtherance of the policies of others.

For a long time the West carried out a policy of containment against China. That policy has ostensibly been dropped but for many in the West the vision of an economically powerful China is frightening. They would rather have an authoritarian Communist China that is economically weak.

I feel it is quite strange that U.S. President Bill Clinton should go to India and Pakistan at the end of his term. The United States is known to disapprove of Pakistan in particular, and also of India. Pakistan and India exploded nuclear devices. At the same time, Pakistan has been condemned for the seizure of power by the military. American Presidents do not usually visit the countries whose policies they disapprove. But apparently this is being done in the context of a bigger foreign policy scenario. It is possible that an attempt is being made to create a power balance in Asia, particularly to curb China. Of course a lame duck President may do strange things as the in-coming Government will not feel itself bound to whatever an out-going President commits himself to.

We in ASEAN (The Association of Southeast Asian Nations) would like India and Pakistan to be at peace with each other. But the Kashmir issue will always stand in the way of good relations between the two. Malaysia does not wish to take sides but we are committed to supporting the UN resolutions on Kashmir. It is expecting too much for two parties to a dispute to resolve it through bilateral negotiations. At some stage a third party must be brought in to arbitrate.

The Kashmir conflict arose historically because of the division of the Indian subcontinent into Pakistan and India. When the ruler of Kashmir failed to join either India or Pakistan, India moved in and claimed a substantial part of Kashmir as Indian territory while Pakistan claimed the rest. However the Kashmir people had not been consulted. Kashmir is a strange state in which the majority of its people were Muslims but the ruler was a Hindu. The Hindu ruler has been removed by India but the people cannot be removed. India and Pakistan may want to make compromises but the people of Kashmir will not allow them to. And so Kashmir will remain a bone of contention between India and Pakistan and it is likely to remain so for a very long time.

China would like to join the World Trade Organisation (WTO). To be a member of the WTO, China must open up its market, a market of 1.3 billion people. At the moment China has a trade surplus with the US and this is something that the US cannot accept. The US can accept even less the growth in China's economic strength. Quite obviously military strength will follow economic wealth. This is what has happened with Japan. When in the immediate post-war years Japan was very poor it was thought that limiting Japan's military expenditure to one percent of GDP would result in Japan being permanently weak. But the Japanese economy grew beyond the expectations of the West and it became the second richest nation in the world. One percent of its GDP spent on the military would be bigger than what the UK spends on arms. Similarly if China becomes rich, even if it spends only a small fraction of its budget on arms, it is going to be very big. This is something that the West will regard with apprehension.

China is also a nuclear power. There is nothing to indicate that it will be less responsible than the Western powers with regard to using nuclear weapons. But then why should it be assumed that Western nuclear powers would be responsible and would not start a nuclear war. The fact is that nuclear weapons, no matter in whose hands they are, make everyone nervous and frightened. Nuclear weapons must be banned for the good of mankind as a whole. For as long as some countries possess nuclear weapons, other countries will try to develop and produce nuclear weapons also. Those with nuclear weapons have no moral right to demand that others should not possess similar weapons.

Malaysia is all for a total ban on nuclear weapons. In fact we are not happy with the continuous upgrading of the lethal qualities of the so-called conventional weapons. The cost of these weapons keep on rising as they get more and more sophisticated. As the rich expand more and more money to develop and produce these weapons they try to recoup their high expenditure by selling these weapons to the countries which are too poor to develop their own weapons. If a country refuses to buy the latest weapons, these will be offered to neighbours or enemies. Scared of the idea of having militarily powerful neighbours and enemies the country has to buy. Then the neighbours will also buy and they will all be accused of having an arms race. And of course all of them will become poorer as they expand such a high percentage of their budget on arms.

Actually what the world needs is not just a ban on nuclear weapons but also a massive reduction in the expenditure on developing new so-called conventional weapons. The world does not need these weapons. They are a waste of money as they bring no return to anyone.

Malaysia is even against nuclear power plants. We don't think that we have complete knowledge about the dangers of using nuclear power. Accidents happen far too ofter. for comfort. The best source of renewable energy is hydro-power. Environmentalists should be more reasonable and accept the need to clear some forests in order to develop hydro-electric plants. This is far better than nuclear power plants of uncertain safety or polluting thermal power plants.

General Pervez Musharraf, the Chief Executive of Pakistan made a working visit to Malaysia on the 27-29 of March. I do not like to comment on the internal politics of other countries but I listened carefully to his account of the circumstances leading to his taking over the Government of Pakistan.

Democracy is the best system of Government that has ever been invented but it is not perfect. Failure to understand the weaknesses and the limitations of democracy by the people will affect its performance adversely. Pakistan has experienced military coups three times. Each time democracy was restored the whole world cheered. But there is nothing to show that Pakistan has done any better as a democracy than it has done under military rule.

General Musharraf promises to return democracy to Pakistan. But he cannot give a date for this to happen because he has to put in place a new system of Government in which the Provinces will have a greater say in provincial governance, reduce corruption and bureaucratic delays and improve the economy. No one can say that all these can be done within a short period of time.

I believe he is sincere in wanting to limit the period of his rule. If everyone, including the political parties cooperate the time taken can be shortened. But if he is not given the political stability needed for his changes to be made, then he may have to stay in power a much longer time. I wish him all the best in his herculean task.

CHAPTER 16

THE MALAYSIAN WAY

I AM MUCH saddened by what has happened to Mr. Obuchi. I think of him as a good friend of Malaysia and also personally. He has succeeded in steering Japan through difficult times more than was expected of him by most people when he was appointed Prime Minister. He has always been able to use his advisers well and that is an essential quality of a good leader. I regret very much that he is not going to be able to represent Japan at the G-8 in Okinawa. I am sure he would be very supportive of ASEAN and the other countries of the South.

During the G77 meeting of the 'South' countries in Cuba, I proposed that the resolutions be transmitted to the G7 as well as the decision that the G77 would not consider any decision by the G7 if the views of the South are not taken into consideration.

There was no suggestion that a representative of the G77 should sit in the deliberations of the G7.

Dust and Humidity

I have been credited with some absurd ideas. It is worthwhile remembering that what was absurd before is commonplace today.

We use vacuum cleaners to suck in dust on the floor. I thought that the same system could be used to suck in air polluted with dust in order to filter it and expel the clean air from the opposite end. Malaysia has high humidity and it seems to me that if the clean air that is about to be expelled is passed over cooling coils it would become drier and reduce sweating and discomfort.

No giant vacuum cleaner is required. A simple ducted fan is all that is necessary. Naturally it will not clean the whole atmosphere. But located at heavily polluted street junctions it can help reduce the dust particles and humidity in the surrounding area.

Apparently the Japanese company I spoke to did not think it was a good idea.

The cause of the spread of Japanese encephalitis in Malaysia has not been fully determined. Some people suggest that it may be due to destruction of the forests. But the disease is more prevalent in areas where there have been no forests. It is fashionable to blame deforestation for everything.

Some people think that I must be working under tremendous stress. Obviously running any country imposes a lot of stress. Some people can handle stress better than others. I think I have an average capacity to work under stress. That it affects me is shown by the heart attack I had in 1989, when I had to be operated on. However I was told that I should not make any decision about retirement immediately after the operation because I was under some post-operative stress.

I am glad I made no decision about retirement at that time. Now I feel capable of carrying on and I do not really feel too much under tension. I have always been able to relax and find sleeping easy. While flying or while being driven to any destination I would doze off and this helps me to recover my strength, both physical and mental. I always snatch a short sleep after lunch while sitting in a comfortable chair.

When currency controls were introduced in September 1998, and then the former Deputy Prime Minister was removed and charged in court, I naturally experienced a lot of tension. But the election proved that the majority of the people are still with the Government.

Although I was convinced that we were right about the controls, there was still a possibility of failure. If we failed, it would damage the whole country and the people. But it turned out that we were right. On many occasions we have to make radical decisions, and we have proven to be right.

You have to be convinced that you are right before you can make a decision. The tension would not be as great as when you are not certain that you are right. However I feel quite relaxed most of the time. Like everyone else I do get sick but nothing so serious as to force me to retire.

I am able to tackle problems methodically partly because of my medical training.

When you encounter some problem, firstly you have to debate within yourself and see how things went wrong. Then, you have to discuss it with others. You have to examine every aspect of the problem. You have to select a group of people who are not afraid to criticise your ideas.

In the case of Malaysia's currency crisis, we set up a Council — which we called the National Economic Action Council (NEAC). The executive committee of this Council met every morning, and discussed the current situation in detail. We argued about how to tackle the problems. Currency controls was my second idea. My first idea which was rejected was to increase the income of everybody and raise the prices of everything in order to neutralise the devaluation. If the value of the currency fell by 100 percent in terms of exchange rate then we raise income by 100 percent. This would result in the purchasing power remaining the same.

But such action has a lot of side effects. While it will help people's ability to buy imports, inflation may become uncontrollable. There are so many things that we cannot predict. My colleagues shot down the plan. So I had to think of other ideas.

We studied currency management in China, Chile, and some other countries. The Malaysian Ringgit had been made freely convertible, which means that currency traders can buy or borrow it freely and indulge in speculation. The result is fluctuations in the exchange rate. A fixed rate can only be made if the currency cannot be traded. Since our exchange rate control we have discovered that apart from China, Argentina and the Caribbean countries have fixed exchange rates; the Caribbean for almost 25 years. We wonder why they are not as viciously attacked as we are for controlling our exchange rate.

In Malaysia, we have been prudent in the management of our finance. We did not borrow too much. We did not use our foreign reserves to defend our currency. We also have lots of liquidity within the system, although at one time money was being siphoned to Singapore. But when we announced that Ringgits not repatriated within one month will not be allowed into the country at all, the money came back, since the money would be useless outside. There are many things that have to be done to tackle economic problems, not just fixing exchange rates.

As a Prime Minister one must think of solutions. Others will also think of possible solutions and come up with ideas. If they come up with a good idea, one must be prepared to consider it. Simply because it isn't one's idea doesn't mean that it is wrong. The only way to succeed is to be able to recognise ideas that are good. If as the Prime Minister I make the wrong evaluation, and the ideas turn out to be bad it will be my responsibility. The ability to evaluate things, and come up with new ideas on your own is very important for leaders.

A leader has to be willing to face criticism and do everything that he can to overcome problems. He has to care about the criticism. If it has a basis, it should be examined. But sometimes, people criticise just because they don't like you. Then, you have to reject such criticism. You cannot be popular all the time. Being criticised is part of the life of a leader. As a leader you are given responsibility by the people. I don't want to leave my office and hand over a country that is in a bad shape. When we want to develop a country we must accept the need to make sacrifices. A nation has to sacrifice a little bit of its environmental quality in order to grow. Pollution is basically due to poverty. If you are poor, you do only those things that you can afford. If you want to clear a piece of land, the cheapest way is to burn the forest. There will be smoke and dust but poor people have to put up with this. It is the rich who complain. When they are inconvenienced they don't think of the problems of the poor.

So, the solution to the environmental problem is actually to enrich the people. In order to enrich the poor people, you must be prepared to buy their products at a high price. If they earn enough it will be easy for the Government to control the trees that they cut. But if their timber is boycotted then they will burn the forests in order to grow other crops. Then there will be pollution and the forests will disappear.

Rich countries must not make the poor countries poorer. If you do they will not be able to look after the environment. Regarding poor countries as the carbon sink of the rich is not the fairest thing to do. It is like asking poor people to remain poor so the rich can enjoy life.

Environmentalists will criticise timber logging companies for making money and being responsible for depleting forest reserves. But they also create employment and pay wages to people who otherwise would have no income. If you force the companies to close down, then they will burn the forest to grow other crops. You will lose timber, you will have pollution, you will lose the carbon sinks.

Rich countries do not even think of these things.

Fortunately for Malaysia, we have other sources of income. Our people are fully employed, we don't have to burn our forests. But in poorer countries, when timber has no value and they want to produce other crops, they burn their forests because that is the easiest way to clear them. Neighbours then have to suffer from haze.

In the long term, the way to avoid this is to enrich the poor. The least that the world community can do is to buy the products of poor countries at higher prices. They can buy processed timber and value-added timber, so that people can become richer. Otherwise they will pollute.

ASEAN (Association of South East Asian Nations) organised the Environment Ministerial Meeting in Brunei last month, which was called the Haze Summit. We tried to discourage forest burning. But it is not easy as people are poor. And recently due to attacks on their currencies the Southeast Asian countries are even poorer. So they will continue to burn their forests to clear the land for food crops.

I attended the G77 Summit in Havana, Cuba, in April. Ideologies are no longer important to these countries. They all want their nations to be more prosperous. All the figures show that over the years, the world's developing nations have been getting poorer. Commodity prices have gone down and more commodities have to be sold by them to buy the same amount of manufactured goods. The goods that they want have risen in price, higher and faster than the rise in price of their commodities. I always believe that if you enrich people, you will become richer yourself. For example, when Japan invests in Malaysia, we became more prosperous and we buy more from Japan thus further enriching Japan. When you impoverish people you destroy your markets.

In the 21st century, technology will change the way of life of people radically. During the Industrial Revolution, the lives of people changed. Instead of working on farms, they went to work in the towns in very bad surroundings and live in poor company houses. Now, we have new technologies, mainly communication technology, i.e. faster movement of information, people and goods. These will also change the lives of people. If you cannot handle these changes, obviously you will not benefit from them. And poor people will be less able to handle these changes.

The early industrialists in Britain produced cotton cloth cheaply, and they flooded India with it. Indian hand weavers went out of business. We fear that such things may happen again. But they need not. Malaysia industrialised by allowing foreign investors in. Poor countries can do this and they will gradually learn the new technology. But the foreign investors must not take everything for themselves. They must leave something for the locals and help them to grow richer. When they are enriched they will be able to buy more from the rich, and the rich can become even richer.

At this moment IT is not doing that. E-commerce companies by selling direct to the consumers in the developing countries will cut out the importers, distributors, and retailers. The consumers may pay less but many people will lose their businesses and workers their jobs. Jobless people cannot buy cheap goods. And Governments will lose revenue. Only the Governments of the rich countries where the dot.com. exporters are located will collect capital gains and corporate taxes.

At the same time we are seeing mega mergers of banks, industries and businesses. When the borders go down these huge corporations will move into the poor countries and swallow up all their companies and banks. These huge corporations will be more efficient, will probably pay better wages. But they will dominate the small countries. We have seen how the small banana-growing countries have become subservient to the great banana plantations owners from abroad. Presently the lenders to the countries impoverished by the deliberate devaluation of their currencies have effectively used the IMF to dominate the countries of their clients. This is wrong. E-commerce should benefit the poor as well as the rich.

Malaysia has set up a body to study globalisation, liberalisation and the borderless world. We think it will have serious consequences for us. That is why we are cautious. To cope we have created the Multimedia Super Corridor. There is nothing anywhere else comparable to Malaysia's Multimedia Super Corridor. A special city will be built for it, which will have its own up-to-date Telecommunication infrastructure. We have created a good environment to live in. Many privileges will be given to those who come in and out of the country to work here. We have attracted 30 world class foreign IT companies as well as nearly 300 IT companies. A multi-media university will produce the needed knowledge workers.

We are developing Kuala Lumpur International Airport as a communications hub. At the same time we are building a new administrative city, a smart city. We are gradually moving into the new administrative city, including my office. These are our responses to the challenge of the IT world. As with our earlier industrialisation, we opened up our country to foreign investors in IT. We hope to benefit from this strategy and eventually to learn enough about IT to use it ourselves for developing our country.

We hope foreign investors, experts and entrepreneurs will come to Malaysia to take advantage of our offer. They will gain much but we will gain too. That is our way, to share what we have with others and to benefit from this sharing through the opportunities that we create. That should be the way for globalisation and the new regime for the world's economy and finances.

CHAPTER 17

THE UMNO SAGA

Q: What is your evaluation of recent UMNO assembly?

A: UMNO meeting was largely supportive of the leadership. There were some unhappiness, but this was due to the lack of understanding. That is why after the explanation was given, the support was strong. They even gave standing ovations twice when I replied to the points they raised. With a party of 2.8 million members, it is sometimes difficult to communicate. Of course loyalties to individuals during the election interfere with the loyalty to the party. But once the election is over UMNO should become stronger.

Q: Why did you stress on money politics?

A: My one great fear is that a leader, especially the Prime Minister of this country will come into power through corruption. That means that corruption will be tolerated by the leadership and everyone will be corrupt. So it is very important that since UMNO leaders will also become government leaders, they should be clean. Everything possible should be done to ensure that only clean leaders should be elected.

Q: It was widely suspected that some of those who won the Vice President seats and Supreme Council seats used money.

A: There are a lot of accusations. But I cannot work on the basis of accusations. I must have clear evidence. I think people did not interpret what they were doing as being corrupt. For example, they say they did not give money to the people who vote as party representatives from the division. They were only giving money to those people who are going to canvas for votes, paying for their travel, hotel for example. They think that is not corruption. To them corruption means giving money to actual voters. They pay their workers because they cannot expect their workers to spend their own money. My view is that even that amounts to corruption. However there are two different periods; one before they gave an undertaking not to campaign and one after they gave the undertaking. Before undertaking not to campaign they were spending money, which lead to accusations of corruption, but after they decided not to campaign at all, no more money was given out. I have to admit though that some of them were believed to continue to use money. I don't know for certain whether those who used money won.

Q: Can you implement more strict regulations in the party, for example prohibit paying the delegates and their family for travel fees, hotel expenses, etc.

A: I will try but it will be very difficult.

Q: Isn't it true that now the Malays are getting richer and this makes them unrespectful of the good values of life?

A: It is natural when a person suddenly gets richer that he loses balance. If you give a million dollars to a poor person, you don't expect him to use it wisely. He will just spend it on anything he likes. That is one of the natural human reaction to sudden wealth. The duty of the Government is to remind the people, to talk to the people that it is not good to do away with good values, such as to know how to be grateful. If you have a sense of gratefulness you will be more responsible. The Government has to revive the culture of the Malays to instill in them good values, not only those which they used to have but also those they didn't have before. It is a process of rebuilding the culture of people.

Q: We the Japanese tend to forget the good values of life. Do you still have some areas that you want to adapt for the Look East Policy?

A: When we first implemented the Look East Policy, the Japanese showed qualities, which were able to overcome the difficulties of the post war years. The Japanese worked hard, were willing even to be paid with just a bowl of rice in order to revive the economy. In the end Japan succeeded. That is the quality that we want to copy; the hard working, dedicated, loyal attitudes of the Japanese workers, and the concerned attitude of the Japanese bosses to the workers. In Japan there is lifetime employment. You don't always do that now. In other countries, they believe that the welfare of the workers is the responsibility of the Government, not the companies. After all they paid tax to the Government. But that kills the loyalty to the company. Without loyalty the company cannot really succeed.

So those were the values that we want to copy. But what we are seeing today, is the result of the exposure of Japanese young people in particular, whose culture is not deeply ingrained. They are exposed to the values that they see in the West. That is why you are seeing irresponsible behavior in Japan. Admittedly you cannot protect your people from outside influence. But every country, which loves its own culture must attempt to deliberately, consciously instill the good values among the younger generation. That is what we want to do in Malaysia.

Q: There are Malay businessmen who only want to rush over profits, and even use your name that "I am very close to the Prime Minister", what do you think?

A: People who have been poor are not too particular about how they can become rich. That is why they use my name. My office has told people that if anybody uses my name, they should check with my office. I don't favour anybody, but when somebody is not fairly treated by the bureaucrats then I will help. What is the good of me being a Prime Minister if I cannot help people?

Q: After the UMNO General Assembly did you decide on your retirement?

A: Frankly I would like to retire as soon as possible. But I also have to be responsible. I just cannot walk out and leave everything in the state of not being prepared for continuing the progress of this country. So whether I like it or not, I have to stay back, and I have to see that the people are in place, who can carry on the work. Of course they may disagree with what I have done. Then they can change after I leave. But I must put the machinery in place to carry on Vision 2020. We have a distinct objective.

Q: What kind of things are left for you to achieve?

A: I think that it is important to a country for the leadership to have ideas. You must come with ideas to progress the country, to solve the problems. And to anticipate changes. That is very important because if you don't come with ideas you cannot develop the country. I still have a lot of ideas on how to develop Malaysia. It is not what I achieve that matters. It is what Malaysia achieves that is important. If I am not the leader I can still do a lot of things.

Q: What kind of problems gives you the biggest headache?

A: The biggest headache comes from trying to balance the development of the indigenous people with the non-indigenous Chinese and Indians. The Chinese are used to urban living, and to wealth. So they are able to deal with prosperity. But the Malays are rural people, very poor people and suddenly they have moved to the towns. In the urban area the life style is different. And they have more money. They cannot handle these changes in a way that is productive. The Government worries that it may lead to a breakdown and failure.

Q: How can you solve this?

A: We have to provide the leadership. We have to provide the right values for them. If necessary we have to talk to different groups of people on the dangers that they face. Maybe they will listen, maybe not. But whether they do or not, we have to try.

Q: Don't the rural people feel the gap between urban people that they are left behind?

A: It is not completely true. If you look at the Malaysian villages today, they are much better than before. You have good roads, electricity, water supply, better houses. They have not been neglected. We have a democratic system, and the opposition is free to spread any amount of lies. They instigate the people. They say that the friends of Prime Minister are very rich. That everyone including the members of the opposition is richer is ignored. Of course each one doesn't get the same amount of benefits. Obviously not everybody will be a millionaire. But the opposition tells the people that all the rich people are friends of the Government in order to make them hate the Government. The rural people are told this even though they themselves do not feel the gap, which separates them.

Q: But if the politician goes to his constituency and talk with the people that will solve a lot of problem.

A: That is totally right. That was what I was saying. They have neglected their duties.

Q: Why did you end your opening speech with prayers?

A: I have tried all kinds of ways to guide UMNO members, particularly with regards to corruption. But still they are easily mislead. So as a last resort I prayed to God.

Q: There is a criticism that your sons sit on many boards as executive in private companies.

A: I know that they are in business and sit on many boards. Many people sit on many boards but that is normal. They are invited to sit because of their experience. They are usually not paid or given privileges as board members. The companies benefit from their experience and know-how, not them.

Q: You have mentioned that PAS is using the mosques for political functions. Do you think that UMNO will go back to stress the importance of religion?

A: We have always stressed the importance of religion. But we have not made use of religion in order to frighten people into supporting us. Instead we preach the brotherhood of Islam as is enjoined by our religion. PAS on the other hand use the mosques to divide the Malays, to create hatred for the Government in order to get votes.

Q: Do you think there is a threat from opposition such as PAS towards the Government? If so, what is it?

A: There is of course a threat. PAS may be able to make Malay Muslims fanatical and to hate us so that they may become violent. But we think we can spread the true teachings about the moderation of Islam and prevent this from happening.

Q: PAS newspaper has been charged? Why is this so and is it against freedom of speech?

A: In Malaysia we have three different races. They used to hate each other and in 1969 there were race riots and more than 100 people were killed. Some newspapers were responsible for instigating race riots and violence. We have to prevent this by requiring newspapers to be licensed. Harakah is licensed as a party paper not for general circulation. It prints lies and tries to stir up hatred between the people. Because of this Harakah must be limited to the same number of issues as other political party papers. It has not been banned.

Q: Now that Mr. Anwar is on trial, is he a threat to you or to the Government? Will he come back to the political scene again?

A: Personally he is not a threat. But the opposition will use his fate to stir up hatred against the National Front in order to get votes. In the 1999 elections, Anwar's "black eye" picture was used successfully to alienate Government supporters.

Q: Why did you have to mention about Mr. Anwar over and over again during the UMNO assembly?

A: I had to mention because many still find it difficult to believe that he committed immoral act. Until they do they cannot be expected to defend the Government convincingly. The truth must be told openly or people will think we are trying to hide things hoping people will forget.

Q: You have also accused Mr. Zahid in your speech, and yet he was elected as a Supreme Council member with a strong support, how do you analyse this?

A: Zahid has recanted and no longer supports Anwar. It is common to welcome back the prodigal son who has admitted that he is wrong.

Q: If you have so many things ahead that means that you cannot step down?

A: I think when major problems are solved I will step down. I cannot say when. Because then it will affect what I want to do to change the atmosphere in the party.

Q: You appointed your successor Mr. Abdullah? How do you evaluate him?

A: We have had four Prime Ministers. Each one had his own style when carrying out basically the same policies. I believe Mr. Abdullah will not change the policies but he will do things his own way.

Q: How do you evaluate yourself?

A: I cannot evaluate myself. It is for others to evaluate. If I do so, it will be biased. Some people want me to stay, some are waiting for me to go. What I think of myself is not important.

Q: I have been doing this interview for almost two years, and I find out that whenever you face serious problem you look younger.

A: Life without problems would be very dull. Problems are exciting challenges. When you solve problems you feel happy and probably look young. I have solved many problems and that may make me look young.

Q: Was these two years the toughest time for you?

A: I must admit that these two years have been one of the toughest time because of a combination of the attack on the economy by outside people over which I had no control; and because Mr. Anwar was found to be not of the right moral character to be my successor. His removal caused a lot of misunderstanding.

Q: It was said that you and Mr. Anwar didn't get along for a long time, after he was in favour of IMF reforms, why did it take almost a year to remove him?

A: I did not agree with his management of the country's finances but I did not agree with him all the time. I could still tolerate him. But when his morals were found to be bad I had no choice but to remove him.

Q: I also found out that the image created by Western media about you is totally wrong. How do you feel being portrayed as dictator? Would you like to change that image?

A: The important thing is what people in this country think of me. As you can see despite the Western media calling me a dictator the Malaysian people gave my party a three-fourth majority. I don't think I can change the image because I will continue to condemn the West and their press if they do anything wrong. They hate me for that. They would like to see me go and so they will always give me a bad image.

Q: Once you have mentioned that you are a doctor so you face people to cure them. Is that why you are weak when it comes to throwing out people?

A: I don't throw out people. I try to work with everyone. People make mistakes but throwing out people does not solve my problem. That is why I never change my staff. I try to get them to do the right thing. If I fail I will try again.

Q: Is it possible that the Prime Minister and UMNO President be a different person?

A: Well it is possible in many countries. The President of the party need not be Prime Minister. On the other hand when you want the party's policy to be followed by the Government, the best thing to do is to have the party's leader as the Government leader. Otherwise there will always be conflicts between the Party's President and the CEO of the Government.

Q: If you say about human factor, is it possible it can happen between you and Mr. Abdullah?

A: I wouldn't know. I think it is possible. I get along with him fine. When you are actually holding an office, you may change. He may change when he becomes the Prime Minister.

Q: You have mentioned that you will devote to party work, and handover work of Prime Minister to your deputy, what kind of work are you going to pass to him?

A: Not all of the work, some of it. I will find somebody else who can do the routine work. I have to look at a lot of papers, meet a lot of people. I might cut down meeting business people. Either I will hand that over to the deputy, or just reduce it. I might reduce visits abroad. He can do some of that, but we will share our work.

Q: What is your evaluation of Mr. Abdullah?

A: He is a good man. He is not the same as me, because no two people are the same. He used to be against me, but as far as I am concerned I don't hold that against him. If you do good for the party, I support.

Q: Why did you decide for him to be the next leader?

A: Well he was one of the Vice Presidents of UMNO. There were three Vice Presidents, one was asked to take leave, the other was perhaps too young. These presidents were chosen by the party. He has a good reputation, and is straight, not trying to grab for power too much.

Q: How do you evaluate the economic situation of Malaysia?

A: The Malaysian economy has turned around, and it is doing very well much better than other countries, which have also turned around. That is because no one with other interest is dictating to us. We have stabilised the currency so that nobody can play around with it. In other countries they are still playing around with the currency. So the freedom to revive the economy is not there. You do something that they consider is against their interest, they will devalue your currency. You will be constrained by this fear. In Malaysia because the currency is fixed and stable, we can do other things, such as reducing interest rates. We can promote sales of property, or of cars. We can help Malaysian companies to recover and so contribute to economic growth.

Q: How is the bank restructuring?

A: We are working on that. It is quite complicated. Malaysian banks are involved in many things, such as brokerage, merchant banking, etc. They also have social obligations. So the banks are not purely commercial in nature. Do we break up the banks, and isolate each function? Do we allow them to go on doing the same things? Anything we do with the banks will disrupt the economy. So we have to be very careful.

Q: Originally the Government announced that all the banks will be merged to six banks, however the idea was changed later.

A: There was a proposal for six banks, but there was a lot of unhappiness among the bankers. The Government is very sensitive to what the private sector thinks. If we find that it is not considered good by them for good reasons, we are quite willing to change. We must keep our ears open. For example, whether it is good to separate banks from brokerage firms. What are the pros and cons? Even with short-term capital flows, we have changed, because we listen to market. We are not rigid. Of course if the market comes up with an idea, which we think is not acceptable, we will reject it. For example they say the Ringgit is too weak and we should allow it to appreciate. We think carefully. At this moment, we don't see any reason for change. We have already said that if our neighbouring countries depreciate or appreciate by 20 per cent, at that stage we will consider whether we will change the exchange rate. We will base changes on our own perception and assessment. At this moment what is wrong with 3.8 Ringgit. Nobody can say it is affecting us very badly. The stock market is doing very well.

Q: Now you have a lot of new political leaders in the world. What do you think is needed for the new world political geography?

A: There should be no rigidity. The old problem was due to rigidity. If you are in the Western camp, even if the Western camp does something wrong, you still support them. If you are in the Eastern camp, you support it without reservation. That is not right. Today I think people are more flexible. If you do something good the people are with you, but if you do something bad, then people will withdraw support from you. Malaysia always support the idea of flexibility. We are not tied to any camp, neither to the East nor the West.

Q: What do you think of the role of NGO and developing countries?

A: Because of their willingness to defy authority and to use violence NGOs can sometimes be more effective than Governments even. Where the developing countries could not stop the WTO from forcing their policies through the NGOs clearly succeeded.

But NGOs representing a small minority negates the rights of the majority. They are therefore an undemocratic force. If the world submits to the NGOs, then there will be anarchy as the NGOs have different and often conflicting agendas. It is difficult to reconcile their struggle for the rule of law through breaking the law. But like the free market the world has come to accept the NGOs and anyone going against them would be considered undemocratic.

Q: How can the small power challenge the gigantic power?

A: If people speak out together, you can achieve something even against the strong. For example the formation of East Asia Economic Caucus (EAEC). How can countries, which form regional organisations like NAFTA deny others the right to form a regional organisation. This is double standard. So we must all stand up and say so. But if we refuse to act together then the strong will always bully us, the weak.

Q: Regarding EAEC, now we have ASEAN + 3, especially in financial field we have recently agreed on currency swap agreement, and this is a drastic change if we think back of 1997 IMF World Bank Meeting in Hong Kong.

A: Yes I totally agree with you. We have made progress. Why

should a country like United States object when we are not doing more than what they are doing. Regarding the currency swap agreement, it is a good beginning. It certainly provides a cushion. In case anything happens, then you can have access to this money. But eventually we should have the Asian Monetary Fund. AMF should be able to monitor the performance of each country and give early warning of what can happen. For example if you adopt a certain policy that is wrong, or the banking system is not functioning properly, AMF should be able to warn and advise. Then you can avoid financial crisis.

CHAPTER 18

JAPAN MUST
REGAIN CONFIDENCE

JAPAN IS THE SECOND biggest economic power in the world after the United States. Yet it is obvious that despite being the biggest donor of foreign aid to developing countries, Japan's role in international affairs, be it political, economic or social is quite insignificant. It would seem that this low international profile of Japan is deliberate.

There is a feeling that Japan fears being accused of having imperial ambitions. During the Pacific War Japan promoted the idea of a Greater East Asia Co-Prosperity Sphere. The Japanese Government and even the Japanese people now want to avoid any suspicion that it wants to revive this concept in whatever form. Indeed the Japanese feel so guilty about their aggression during the Pacific War that they feel a need to apologise even now, more that half a century after.

Coupled with this guilty feeling is a desire not to offend the victors, in particular the United States. In so far as being no longer aggressive and militaristic is concerned, this is welcome by Japan's Asian neighbours. Even Japan's acceptance of democracy and no longer treating the Japanese Emperor as a god but merely as a constitutional monarch is reassuring to East Asians in particular. It is about time for Japan to take an independent stand and state its views clearly without having to fear the U.S. For example no real progress has been made in the Okinawa G8 Summit. There was still opposition from United States and Britain regarding restructuring the financial regime and debt forgiveness for least developed nations. Instead the emphasis is still on strengthening the IMF. We know Japan wants to do more for a better world but it seems to bow to the wishes of others.

Of late we are seeing an attempt to fully Westernise every aspect of Japanese society, particularly Japanese management of its economy and Japanese business practices. After decades of doing things the Japanese way, and doing very well indeed, now quite suddenly the Japanese want to change and do everything the Western way. Worse still the change is to be effected immediately at any cost. Even here Japan is adopting the 'big bang' approach, an approach that is unhealthy for anyone.

Japan's economy and industrial capacity was totally destroyed by the War. But as we all know Japan recovered very quickly to become the second biggest economy in the world. Japan was able to do this because of very close working relations between the Government and the business sector, which earned Japan the title, Japan Incorporated.

This cooperation ensured that Japan's resources were well distributed and waste avoided. The Yen which depreciated during the war was not revalued. Although this made Japan's imports costly and Japan had to import most of the raw materials required for its industries, it made Japanese exports very competitive. This earned Japan the foreign exchange that it needed to revive its economy.

The Zaibatsu was broken up but the companies of the same group continued to work closely together. Each group had its own bank and this helped access to necessary capital. Effectively the Zaibatsu survived but each of the companies, which resulted from the break-up became as big or even bigger than the original Zaibatsu. And they all contributed to the rapid economic growth of Japan, at times with double-digit figures.

While the developed countries of the West became worried about Japan's recovery and growth and the increasing trade deficits suffered by the West, the developing countries benefited from the cheap high quality goods streaming out of Japan.

Japanese business strategy differed from that of Western businesses. The Japanese went for market share through high volumes and low margins. The developed industrialised countries of the West went for high margins and looked mainly at the developed markets. They did not really design their products and prices for the developing countries. Had they been the sole producers of manufactured goods, particularly consumer products, the poor countries would not be able to afford modern necessities and luxuries.

Developing countries would not have been able to buy manufactured goods especially when commodity prices kept going down relative to the prices of manufactured goods. But the low priced Japanese goods enabled poor people in poor countries to buy some of the motor vehicles and household appliances Japan produced.

But there are other benefits for some developing countries. In order to compete with the Japanese, Western countries invested in manufacturing facilities in developing countries, increasing employment and development. More importantly it banished forever the belief among many Asians that manufacturing sophisticated products is beyond them. With increasing self-confidence these countries began to industrialise on their own until the West feared that there would emerge many new Japans which would push them out of the market altogether.

The Japanese work ethics is another great contributor to the recovery of Japan. Japanese companies were essentially family-initiated and family-controlled companies. There may be public shareholders but management remains largely in the hands of the family.

More than that the owners regard the employees as members of their families almost. Unlike Western companies which sack employees if losses are incurred, Japanese companies keep their employees even during bad times. And they continue to look after their employees even after retirement.

Naturally employee loyalty and dedication is very strong and this contributed towards higher productivity. While professionals have a place in the management of Japanese companies, family members retain the control over management. Managers usually rise from the ranks and have been in the company for decades before becoming executives. Outsiders are never brought in to manage even though they may have a reputation for management skills of a high standard.

All these practices are especially peculiar to Japan and the Japanese and without doubt they had contributed to Japan's economic success. This is recognised by Japan's competitors. If Japan is to be curbed, these Japanese practices must be stopped.

The close cooperation between the Japanese Government and Japanese business which was given the sobriquet Japan Incorporated was condemned. According to Japan's Western rivals this was unethical. Governments should never cooperate with the private sector.

They should instead put bureaucratic obstacles in the way of private businesses.

This condemnation should be accepted if the accusers are free from such practices. But Japan must know that the Western countries are equally guilty of cronyism, the 'old school tie' and nepotism.

When Malaysia was a British colony, the British Government imposed a policy called Imperial Preference to ensure that only goods produced by British companies were bought by the Malaysian colonial Government and others. Even after Independence in 1957 Malaysia followed this policy. Only in 1968 was the first Government supply contract given to a Japanese firm.

That was before. But is it still true that Western Governments work closely with the private sector? We know of the massive subsidies given by these Governments for many industries, for new start-up industries and for agricultural products. Governments send their ministers abroad to lobby for contracts for their companies, and often offer loans for unrelated matters in order to sweeten the offers.

The support given by Western Governments to hedge funds is well-known, in particular the Long-Term Credit Management Fund (LTCM) which would have gone bankrupt if the Government had not forced banks to lend to LTCM.

The ideas about globalisation, liberalisation, deregulation, transparency etc are hatched by the private sector in the West and their Governments pushed them through using persuasion and threats in a way that is worse than Japanese private/public sector cooperation which is mainly domestic. The idea of the WTO is nothing more than an effort by the Governments to support their private sector.

All these things are being done by the very people who condemn Japan Incorporated. But they have managed to make it out that their Government/private sector collaboration is right, but similar practices by the Japanese are wrong. And today we are seeing the Japanese feeling guilty about Japan Incorporated to the extent that civil servants fear to have anything to do with businessmen. The fear is real as several senior civil servants were arrested for doing nothing more than what they had always been doing.

Japan has subscribed fully to the floating exchange rate. The floating rate is acceptable if it is truly market forces which determine the Yen-Dollar exchange rate. But the Plaza Accord had nothing to do with market forces. It was a political decision made largely because Japan's trade rivals wanted to reduce the competitiveness of Japan.

The currency trading by hedge funds also cannot be described as a market force. Currency traders with billions of Dollars can push the Yen up or down by buying or selling. Only the Japanese Government has enough resources to counter the traders. But intervention by the Government bank is regarded an interference with the market and is objected to. And so the Japanese Yen has appreciated to the detriment of the Japanese economy and incidentally making life difficult for the poor countries.

The Japanese say they can adjust to the strong Yen but that adjustment will affect the rate of recovery for Japan and also the recovery of many other countries for whom cheap Japanese goods mean higher living standards.

If the Yen is properly managed it will contribute towards rapid recovery for Japan. But Japan is still unwilling to allow trade settlement in Yen or to deposit Yen in countries which need it most. Instead it is being used to support the rich and the powerful. Japan will not control the Yen and its appreciation or depreciation will adversely affect Japanese recovery. Only a steady exchange rate can hasten economic recovery anywhere, even in Japan.

Japanese companies are still bringing out an endless range of new products including motorcars. They should all be doing well. But instead they are failing and they are throwing out their employees on the streets.

The reason is this desire to adopt Western business practices. Families must give up their management control over their companies and hand them over to professional managers.

Some professional managers may be good but they are no guarantee of success. Professional managers do not have the same love for the company even if they hold shares and stock options. Their main interest is to show their ability to push up quarterly profits in order to make shareholders happy and be willing to reward the executives further.

They may do this by not reinvesting. Even then they will have no hesitation about leaving the company if they get better offers. If the company fails they will still get good compensation through a golden handshake which they had arranged for themselves.

I am not sure that professional management will be good or bad for Japanese companies. But I am certain that the turmoil that the change in system will cause will be bad for them. If the system has to be changed, a gradual process would cause less disruption and damage than a 'big bang'. But why change when you were doing well with your old private ownership and management and cradle to the grave support for your employees?

In the interest of Japan, in the interest of East Asia and indeed in the interest of the world, we need a politically stable and economically healthy Japan. Since Japan is a democracy it is for the Japanese people to bring about these things. By all means espouse and even glorify democracy. It is the best system of governance ever developed by Man. But it is important to remember that it is not without defect. Wrongly practised it can cause as much damage as any other system of governance.

Democracy was invented because of the need for an equitable and just society. To achieve this there must be peace and stability. Unfortunately what we are seeing today is not what democracy was meant to achieve. Very often we are seeing lawlessness, instability and economic and social regression caused by abuses of democracy in the name of democracy. And because it is in the name of democracy we may not reject whatever is being done even when it destroys us.

It is the same with many things which are being done in the name of the free market, universal values, transparency etc. The objectives do not matter as long as the means are right and proper.

Japan's success has inspired Asians. But now the Japanese have lost confidence in themselves. They have rejected almost everything that is Japanese in an apparent desire to be accepted by the West. In the process they have weakened themselves and in many instances they have failed.

Because of the economic crisis, companies have been taken over by foreign companies, and the culture has changed inside the companies. The businessman are not used to it and lost their dignity. I think they can rebuild in a small way, instead of thinking about shame. Let's have confidence and start all over again. I know that the Japanese can do it. Start rebuilding small business, take advantage of modern technology. Now even big business depends upon outsourcing parts. They should go into an area where they are good. There is also good sign in the new Japanese generation. They are venturing into new and innovative IT based businesses on their own. They avoid employment in the big Japanese companies. But they must also realise that the success rate in the new business is very low. Only one in 10 or in 100 will succeed. If they fail, they may think that the world is not good. They might get bitter and frustrated.

Whereas in Malaysia where Muslims are devoted to their religion, the Japanese don't have one specific religion to identify with themselves. Still you have good family values which you should stay with. Family values are very important. When I was in Japan recently, I heard about lots of murder cases, bus jack etc among youngsters which I did not expect. Japanese youth should have something healthy and active to fill the time. If they have idle time, then they will be occupied with useless activities. You should have some aim in life or belief, whether it is religion or patriotic belief. You have to have a belief in something.

Still Japan had managed to remain the second largest economy in the world. You have achieved the goals that you set. You are not hungry anymore. Your people lost enthu-siasm and your dreams for the future. It is like the period of decline of the Roman Empire. In European history not a year passed without wars. Every twenty years they fought major wars. It concentrated their energies and directs their feelings against their enemies. It left them little time for destructive activities within their own societies. Now they experience half a century without war. It destabilises them. They must seek enemies to defeat. If it is not a military conquest then it must be ideological or economic.

But idleness and prosperity have the same effect on other people too. Japanese young people are also prone to thrill-seeking because of this. It is better to keep them occupied with something worthwhile. They should once again experience the hardships of poverty by going to live for short periods in the least developed countries among the poor. They will then understand the difficulties of life and they will learn to contribute to the well-being of others. They will have something useful to do and life for them would no longer be empty of challenges. They will go home with a better understanding of the world and the constructive role they can play.

I also worry about what is happening with incidents that your country never had before. For example, the Snow brand milk poisoning, nuclear plant leak, etc. If you compare with Malaysia, everything is expensive in Japan, especially products like beef, melon, cherries, etc. People are willing to pay absurd prices thinking that it is safer and better than imported goods. But this is not true any longer. In the past when the Japanese do something, you used to do it very, very carefully, step by step. Now it seem to me that you don't care anymore whether it is good or bad. The old spirit and values are not there anymore. The Japanese culture is changing too rapidly. People have lost their direction. Before it was very simple and easy; import raw material, add value and export. You were good in manufacturing. Now raw materials don't mean so much to you. Like the Europeans you have become inventors and innovative. As a result you have become move individualistic and the community and nation mean less to you now. You don's mind selling off your great corporations to foreigners and work for them in your own country. However for many Japanese this is something that he cannot adjust to.

Asians look at what is happening in Japan with dismay. The Japanese people must pull themselves together and reassert their faith in their system and values. Japan must recover and recover quickly.

This can only happen when the Japanese people realise that Japan needs a strong Government which can act decisively to restore the belief in the Japanese way of doing things. Japan must never again entertain territorial ambitions or even economic hegemony, but a stable and prosperous Japan taking its proper leadership role in the community of nations, speaking up for the poor and the oppressed, contributing to their development will be welcomed, admired and emulated. In time even its rival will be appreciative of its contribution to prospering the world.

Leaders should not think in terms of becoming Prime Minister for two years, as some kind of decoration. They must think in terms of having a Prime Minister for a sufficient length of time for him to be able to deliver. He may not be a great leader but even a great and brilliant person cannot do anything in two years. You would be too worried about your position and would concentrate on politics, not on administering the country, solving its problems and prospering it.

I also think it is important for Japanese to be more frank when dealing with others. We are never certain of what the Japanese really mean when they say something. Even when they say 'yes' to something, it may not mean 'yes'. This makes relations between Japan and other countries difficult.

Yet Japan, because of its wealth and technology, its great skill must be a leader of the region. Leaders must be easily understood and Japanese ambivalence and ambiguity make Japanese leadership difficult to accept. Asians look up to Japan and the Japanese. But so far you have not lived up to their expectations as a friend and a leader.

I write as the citizen and leader of a small country which has many reasons to be thankful to Japan.

INDEX

DR MAHATHIR MOHAMAD, one of the most durable and outspoken figures on the world political stage, has been prime minister of Malaysia since July 16, 1981. He first came to prominence in 1969 when he was expelled from the ruling party, UMNO, for writing a letter critical of the then prime minister, Tunku Abdul Rahman. Before being readmitted to UMNO in 1972, he wrote his famous, highly controversial work, *The Malay Dilemma*, which examined the economic backwardness of the Malays, and advocated state intervention to bring about their rehabilitation. The book was promptly banned in Malaysia. In *The Challenge* (1986), he explodes fallacies and exposes distortions concerning religion, education, democracy, Communism, freedom and discipline, and the concerns of this world and the next. In *A New Deal for Asia* (1999), Dr Mahathir reflects on Malaysia's fight for independence and rails against those who blindly worship the free market.

As Malaysia's fourth prime minister, Dr Mahathir has played a pivotal role in the confident march of his people towards Vision 2020, his blueprint for Malaysia's advance towards fully developed status. Born on December 20, 1925, Dr Mahathir studied medicine in Singapore, where he met his future wife, Dr Siti Hasmah Mohd Ali. After working as a doctor in government service, he left to set up his own private medical practice in his hometown, Alor Setar. In 1974, he gave that up to concentrate on his political career. Dr Mahathir and his wife have seven children and ten grandchildren.

what they say about
A New Deal for Asia

"... Dr Mahathir Mohamad's *A New Deal for Asia* is a practical book. It shows a practical man with practical ideas applicable not just for Asia but for the rest of the world." *The Sun*

"As we pick up the pieces, Dr Mahathir's book is timely reading. Those of us who did not want to hear him speak up at that time for fear of further fluctuation in the value of the ringgit, would appreciate his reasoning now." *The Star*

"... a chastening read ... Dr Mahathir says much that needs to be said. ... [He] is about the only leader of a democratic, developing country who has the mettle to contradict the big powers. Where others waffle, he cuts to the quick. ... He says publicly what many leaders think, but don't have the guts to enunciate. ... The book's strength is the long section dealing with Malaysia's seemingly inexorable rise during the 1980s and 1990s—and its abrupt fall due to the Crisis. And he is largely right. Indeed, the evidence for his argument grows as time passes. His attacks on the IMF were initially ridiculed as the rantings of a man who was a few sandwiches short of a full picnic. Then others began to echo his criticisms, until the IMF acknowledged a 'slight mistake'. ... he is worth listening to and he does provoke. [His] capacity for provocation is perhaps his greatest attribute." *Asiaweek*

"For those who vehemently opposed Malaysian Prime Minister Mahathir Mohamad's world view, don't expect his book to be any sort of deviation. For those who consider his anti-Western convictions vindicated by the Asian economic crisis, *A New Deal for Asia* offers a timely and readable reaffirmation. ... What comes through loud and clear is Mahathir's utter dismay at the power of global economic sentiment, and his unflinching belief that Malaysia and the rest of Asia are victims of a new form of imperialism." *Far Eastern Economic Review*

"... we should seek truth from experience, and as we can't always trust the filters of either the local or foreign press, I would recommend that Dr Mahathir's *A New Deal for Asia* is worth picking up." **Men's Review**